I. O. W. SECTION
1ST JANY 1930.

Y

S

ENGINE NUMBERS															TOTAL Nº OF ENGINES
															2³
															I
															I
															I
23	24	25	6	27	28	29	30	31	32						614
															I
															I
															2 I

TOTAL NUMBER OF ENGINES 23

26

	25	DSHILL.
	26	ITWELL.
	27	ERSTONE.
ALL	28	HEY
EW	2C	LVERSTONE
WOOD	30	SHORWELL.
RNE	31	CHALE
NKLIN	32	BONCHURCH.
DOWN		
ADING.		
LAND.		
BOURNE.		

S.R. (S W SECTION)
C.M.E. DEPT
DRAWING OFFICE
EASTLEIGH

R.E.L. MAUNSELL.

Nº E 19200

MacLeod's Other Island

The story of the Southern Railway's first Assistant for the Isle of Wight

By
Terry Hastings and Roger Silsbury

Published by
The Isle of Wight Railway Co. Ltd.

© Isle of Wight Railway Co. Ltd., Terry Hastings & Roger Silsbury

British Library Cataloguing in Publication Data
A record for this book is available from the British Library

ISBN 978-0-9506154-5-5
Published by: Isle of Wight Railway Co Ltd, The Railway Station, Havenstreet, Isle of Wight, PO33 4DS
Typesetting and Photo Restoration by: Holne Publishing Services, PO Box 343, LEEDS, LS19 9FW
Printed by: Cambrian Printers, Llanbadarn Road, Aberystwyth, Ceredigion, SY23 3TN

Reasonable efforts have been made to discover the true copyright owners of the photographs reproduced in this volume, and no infringement of copyright is intended. If you have any evidence about the copyright owner of any photograph, or the photographer of any photograph listed as 'photographer unknown', please contact the publisher in the first instance.

Photographs in this volume have been digitally adjusted to enhance clarity, and also remove blemishes, dust etc. However, no intentional alterations have been made to affect their historical significance.

Isle of Wight Railway Co. Ltd.
The Railway Station,
Havenstreet,
Isle of Wight,
PO33 4DS

Cover Photos:
Front Cover:
Top Left: W24 *Calbourne* at Ryde St Johns Road in ex-works condition 1933.   (Photo: A.B.MacLeod collection)
Top Right: Alistair Balmain MacLeod, 1932, in a portrait by photographer Eleanor Churchill.
(Photo: E.MacLeod collection)
Bottom: MacLeod Tartan and Crest. (E.MacLeod collection)

Back Cover:
The Isle of Wight Steam Railway is recreating the past glory of the Island's railways and the rear cover illustrations seek to show how close to authenticity it is able to get, using appropriately liveried and matched stock.
Top: Class A1X W8 *Freshwater* with LCDR pull and push set 484 heads a Ventnor West service on 10th October. Was it 1933 or 2010? The low evening light highlights all the vehicles to perfection.   (Photo: John Faulkner)
Bottom: 18th September and an early morning Cowes to Ryde Pier Head train hauled by Class O2 W24 *Calbourne* and comprising two SECR and one LBSCR carriages climbs towards Ashey. It could easily be 1950, not sixty years later.
(Photo: John Faulkner)

Contents

Above: A chalked advertisement at Newport station. By, or at, MacLeod's request? (Photo: A.B.MacLeod)

Introduction

The Museum of the Isle of Wight Steam Railway has for many years been custodian of a fine archive of Island artefacts and photographic material. This resource has, in recent years, been used extensively by authors and historians and through their publications much has been put into the broader public domain.

More recently the Museum seized an opportunity to acquire a collection of more than 500 photographs once belonging to Alistair MacLeod. Many of the views were familiar but what was of particular interest were the annotations on the reverse: names, dates and general information which had hitherto been missing or only guessed at!

There is also a considerable archive of documentation relating particularly to the mid-Southern Railway period on the Island. To celebrate 40 years since the founding of the Isle of Wight Steam Railway Museum we have gathered together what we hope is an intriguing and informative selection of MacLeod related items. It must be remembered however, that MacLeod's pictures were originally taken for his own interest and the quality can be variable but are a fascinating insight into his world. The authors make no apologies for reproducing some less than perfect, but unique, views.

Alistair MacLeod was the charismatic manager of the Island's railways during one of the most dramatic periods of development. He arrived in 1928 and was responsible for implementing an array of improvements, as a result of which his name became near legend. Whilst researching for this book, it became abundantly clear that there was also a personal story to tell. In consequence we have included narrative from both interviews and written sources with friends and family, and perhaps as importantly from MacLeod himself. It is our hope we shed a little more light on the man and his work than hitherto published - possibly more fact and a little less of the fiction!

The MacLeod Clan's ancestral home is on the Isle of Skye and this naturally held a place dear to Alistair's heart, but after only a couple of years he was surprised to find that the Isle of Wight had become a major rival for his affections, becoming 'The Other Island'. Eventually leaving for career reasons, this Island still remained the base for family holidays for three generations.

It would be nice to think that this publication may inspire another author to write a full biography. This work we intend as a celebration of the time and influence on the railways of the Isle of Wight by Alistair Balmain MacLeod, A. M. I. Mech. E., M. I. Loco. E., M. Inst. T.

Terry Hastings
Roger Silsbury
July 2011

Chapter One
Family and Friends

Above: Dr John MacLeod
(Photo: E.MacLeod collection)

Dr John M.H.MacLeod was the son of a General Practitioner in Dundee. After education at the Universities of St Andrews and Aberdeen as well as Paris, Hamburg and Vienna he finally settled in London, setting up practice as a skin specialist. He married Eva in 1897 and on 24th January 1900 Alistair Balmain MacLeod was born.

The family home was 'above the shop' at No 11, Harley Street and in 1905 Alistair was joined by a sister Rona. Their childhood was stated by Alistair as comfortable and happy but well ordered-children were seen but not heard during surgery hours.

Enrolled in nearby Miss Gough's kindergarten in Marylebone High Street, Alistair was soon rubbing shoulders with the great and mighty. Ewan MacLeod, his son, tells the story, *"One rainy day he trudged home sharing an umbrella with a pretty girl called Betty. Her full name was Elizabeth Bowes-Lyon, and on the year they both became octogenarians, Alistair penned a reminder with his birthday card to H.M. The Queen Mother!"*

Further education followed at Fairfield Preparatory School at Malvern Link, and later, during World War One, at Cheltenham College. There was also during this period attendance at a crammer in Windermere.

Cluttering the floor with his model railway and expressing a great interest in matters mechanical was a clear indication to the family that Alistair was likely to break with their medical traditions. MacLeod's spare time was taken with train-spotting around the Capital and he was,

Above: Fairfield Preparatory School, Malvern Link, in 1911. A.B.MacLeod is seated left of master Mr Capel Smith.

(Photo: E.MacLeod collection)

Left: A proud Alistair at 14 years displays model locomotives from his collection. The two tender engines sold by Bassett-Lowke were named *George the Fifth* and *Queen Mary* and built by either Bing or Carette. The L&NWR tank engine was also retailed by Bassett-Lowke and possibly built by Carette.
(Photo: E.MacLeod collection)

Right: Alistair and sister Rona at Kelham Hall in 1919.
(Photo: E.MacLeod collection)

after some resistance, finally allowed to construct a model railway on trestles in the attic.

Ewan MacLeod asks, *"Where did this interest come from? Presumably a gene inherited from his mother, who was the daughter of Joseph Ruston of Lincoln, one of the founders of the great engineering firm of Ruston & Hornsby."*

Alistair was called up in September 1918, posted to the Royal Fusiliers and, as a private, deployed in the 3rd Reserve Battalion R.E. at Kelham Hall, Newark-on-Trent.

During this period he occupied his time drawing and remodelling 'O' gauge locomotives and his cloth-bound volume of signed scale drawings from this date remains a fascinating and treasured family item which few have been privileged to see.

Demobilised in February 1919, Alistair faced his career choice; whilst his parents were well-connected he almost certainly had multiple options but was told by his father to get a job pronto! Alistair first spent a brief period with a local firm learning carpentry and soldering, skills which served him well with his modelling, as we shall see.

Above: A page from one of Alistair MacLeod's albums, the notes are in his own hand.

(Photo: E.MacLeod collection)

Soon after he took up a position as an Articled Pupil at the London, Brighton & South Coast Railway (LBSCR) works in Brighton. This was partly under the tutelage of Locomotive Superintendent L.H.Billinton, whilst other areas included operation of running sheds, workshop training and drawing office experience. MacLeod's training paid dividends and in 1923 he was appointed Assistant District Locomotive Superintendent at Brighton, moving on in 1925 to the position of Assistant to Eastern Divisional Locomotive Running Superintendent at Waterloo for the new Southern Railway (SR).

(E/92/43)

LONDON BRIGHTON & SOUTH COAST RAILWAY.

No. 67

PASS

TO RIDE ON LOCOMOTIVE ENGINE.

Brighton, 10th July 19

Issued to Mr McLeod

Available ~~until~~ 10th & 11th July 1919.

L Billinton per

Loco.-Engineer.

Engs 327, 328, 19, 25, 81, 572

N.B.—Before this Pass can be used the Holder must sign the declaration on BACK.

Waterlow & Sons Limited, Printers, London Wall, London.

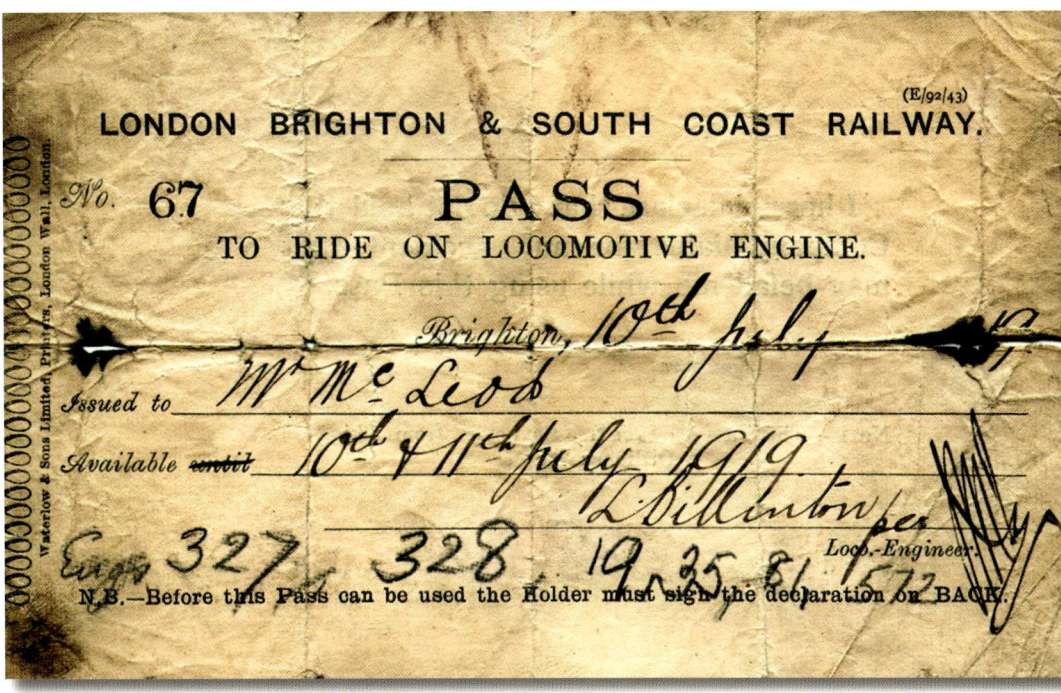

Before we move on to Alistair's railway activities in the Isle of Wight, his son Ewan MacLeod provides a little more background to his father's early years:

"Father obtained a comprehensive practical training and very quickly started up the ladder of responsibility. He learned the art of firing and did numbers of runs in that duty, culminating in at least one run on 'Gladstone', No.214 from Brighton to London.

The skill he acquired was also put to good use throughout his life when he took many opportunities to drive recreationally on private lines. Visits to a house owned

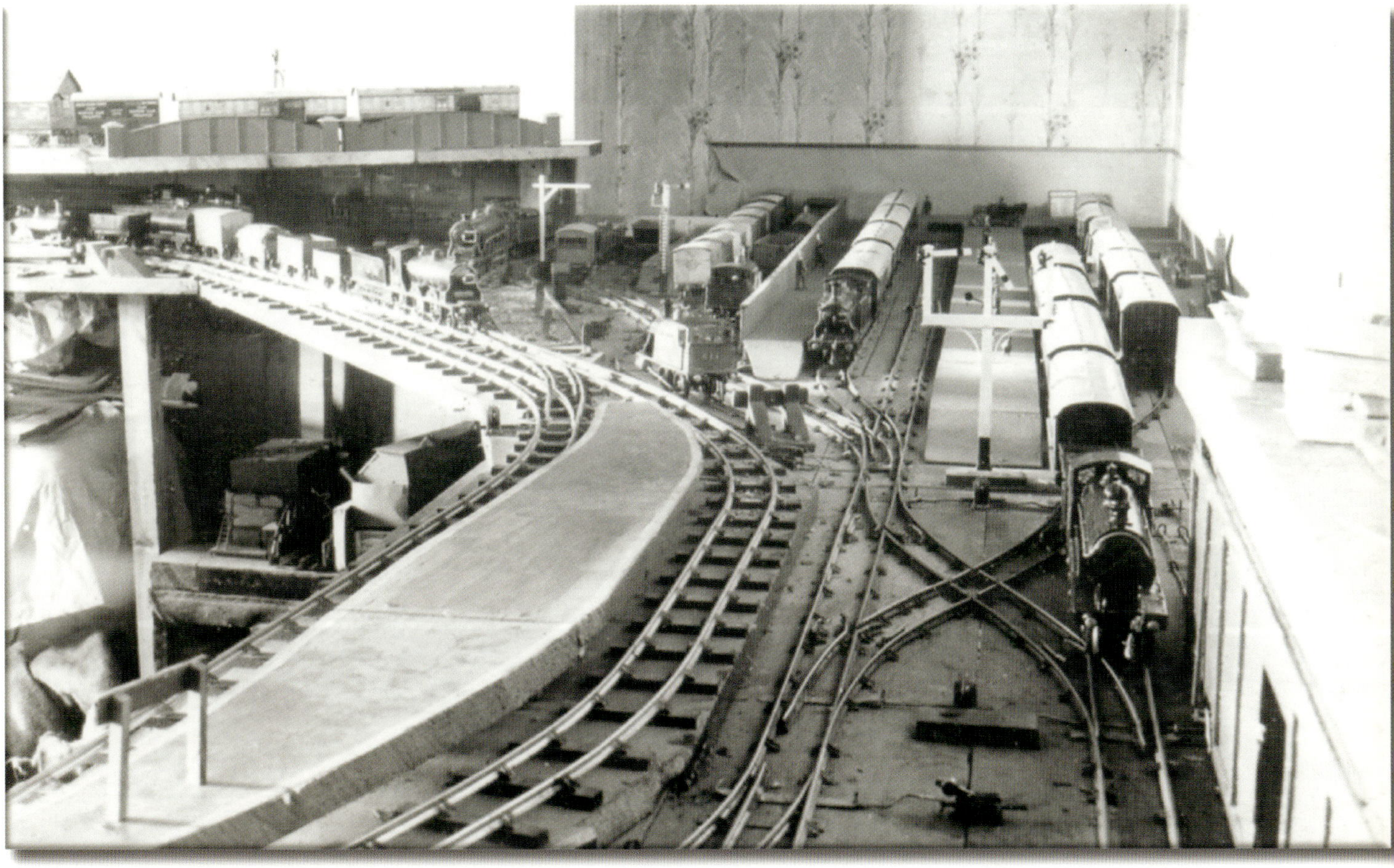

Above: 'Carlisle' station in the upper rooms of 11, Harley Street in the 1920s. (Photo: E.MacLeod collection)

Left: During his apprenticeship, Mac, seen as fireman, looking from the cab of LBSCR class E4 No.485 at Brighton waiting to work a goods to Tunbridge Wells in the 1920s. (Photo: E.MacLeod collection)

Below: Mac at the controls of RHDR's 1931-built Canadian replica locomotive No.10 *Doctor Syn* in 1955.   (Photo: E.MacLeod collection)

Right: Fashionable twenty-somethings, Winifred and Alistair on the steps of St John's, Smith-square, Westminster on the occasion of their marriage on Saturday 23rd February 1928.

(Photo: E.MacLeod collection)

Mr. A. B. MacLeod and Miss Winifred Bray

The marriage between Mr. Alistair Balmain MacLeod, only son of Dr. and Mrs. J. M. H. MacLeod, of 11, Harley-street, W., and Miss Winifred Bray, younger daughter of Lieutenant-Colonel R. E. T. Bray, late Royal Berkshire Regiment, and of Mrs. Bray, of 34, Westminster-mansions, and Littlestone, Kent, and granddaughter of the late Sir John Barwick, Bart., took place, very quietly, at St. John's Church, Smith-square, Westminster, on Saturday morning.

by his future wife's family at Littlestone-on-Sea introduced Alistair to the 15" Romney, Hythe & Dymchurch Railway (RHDR), where he met Jack Howey. Years later after World War Two he assisted Capt. Howey get the line back on its feet and became an official 'guest driver' for several years, clocking up over 3000 miles in RHDR service.

Brighton days were also the crucible for many railway acquaintanceships which prospered through the years. M.S.Hatchell (Monty) became a lifelong friend with whom Alistair later shared lodgings and the construction of several 'O' gauge model railways. In the meantime Brighton weeks were punctuated by London weekends and the attic layout in Harley Street expanded. To overcome a structural impediment a tunnelled exterior loop was built to link two windows and great excitement was caused when a cat took up residence and was struck at speed by a model of 'The Great Bear'.

Alistair, Monty and two others from Brighton made a noteworthy journey in 1927 when one weekend they travelled from King's Cross to Inverness and back to Euston, some 1230 miles in 33 hours. It was at a time when the Big Four were still grappling with the integration of their many forebears and the great attraction was the many engine changes needed, 12 in all during the trip."

In addition to Monty, Alistair was joined on the trip by Patsy Carré from the Iron Foundry and A.J.Hollins of the Drawing Office. A detailed log of the journey and a very amusing four-page narrative by the man himself records the whole journey in what is best described as 'Olde English'! Many years later, friend Ian Allan sanitised the whole affair and published it in *Trains Illustrated*....it really lost a great deal in translation!

In due course Alistair found himself at Waterloo and married to Winifred Bray on Saturday 23rd February 1928.

The ceremony took place 'very quietly' in the beautiful English Baroque masterpiece that is St John's, Smith-square, Westminster. Surprisingly for the surroundings, lounge suits were the order of the day. Soon, fortune took them to the Isle of Wight and "the finest job in the world". As might be expected a model railway was quickly established in their first Island home in the upper floors of a house in Ryde's East Hill Road; the MacLeod apartments were known as *The Rookery*; subsequently the whole building was named *Argosy* and still survives. This was not to be a long stay and family, together with railway, were transferred to *Olga House*, on the seafront at Springvale. From the evidence, the railway was clearly a sectional beast and was easily demounted and reconstructed with suitable amendment at almost any location.

Son Ewan, born in London, was followed by daughter Alison, born on the Island and the family enjoyed three glorious years during which Alistair, apart from almost total commitment to his work, became an enthusiastic dinghy sailor at the Seaview Yacht Club, a freemason in Ryde Lodge No.698, a director of the Southern Vectis Bus

Around the United Kingdom in Forty Eight Hours.

An Oddessey in several Acts.

It chanced upon a time that four goodly persons of this fayre land did feel the spirit of adventure upon them and did fair forth for to examine and explore that savage part of our realm known as Scottelande. And so upon the seventeenth day of June Anno Domini 1927 they did betake themselves to the station which is called Kynge's Crosse and did there embark upon the train called "Aberdonian."

Now a goodly crowde of persons had assembled to bid them farewell and while one did speak in a foreign language another was revealed as one of the principal seneschals of the Southern Railway. and all were of good cheer and merrie. And the train did start at 7.30 pm. and the Evening and the Morning were the first day.

And passing through the Tunnel which is called Copenhagen a greate cloude of foul gas did assail their nostrils and was nigh to exterminate the party by reason of the foul stench. but coming presently to thr open air, the travellers made shift to revive themselves and after one of them had spent a lengthy time in washing they did repair to the Car of Dining where a goodly feast was eaten. All were again merrie but another attack of gas, this time on the part of the Outdoor Machinery Dept of the S.R. did temporarily place their spirits in a downward direction for several pegs. After two of the travellers didi seek to consume smoke from the oft folled leaves of Havana, but as chance has it Nature very nearly did her worst and only timely shots through the open portal did forestall a catastrophe.

And now the town of Grantham drew near and was reached a full minute before the appointed hour and the subsequent course to York was also traversed with great expedition. And about this time a hounde did begin to manifest itself and was greatly beloved by most of the party, but to one of them he made no appeal, in that the nose of him should not have been coloured red as Nature had seen fit to do.

But the world is ever a bundle of hay, And now did the party compose itself for slumber, but with little success for our steed, the "City of Ripon" did move itself with belated steps and there was murmuring among the people. But eventually it was New Castle and the Evening and the Morning were 1.16 am.

And now did that noble horse "W? Whitelaw " appear upon the scene and another attempt was made to woo sweet Mistress Sleep but t'was vain for the Leader of thre party did give vent to his feelings in no uncertain manner and all were merrie. But on a time peace wafted her sweet wings through the compartment and slumber (Of a sort) reigned for at least an hour and a half. And now behold the Town of Edinburgh drew nigh and soon the panting steed (Westinghouse Combination Valve) came to a stand at the well known hostelry of Waverly. And the time it was on the tick, and the Evening and the Morning were to-morrow.

Above: An extract from the historic journey to 'Scottelande' in 1927.
(E.MacLeod collection)

Co. and involved with many Island personalities and Island matters, including the Ryde Amateur Players. In April 1932 they produced Arnold Ridley's *Ghost Train* at the Theatre Royal in Ryde and the programme contains the special mention of Mac thanking him for '*preparation of the necessary effects*'; one wonders exactly what he provided...the local press report appears to focus on this aspect perhaps to the detriment of the players who were certainly shunted into a siding!

Olga House, which still looks out across the water towards Spithead, was an ideal location for viewing the many transatlantic liners of those days. Mac took many photographs, even recording some really rough winter days when water crashed over the sea wall onto the front of the house, and, in summer, wife Winifred inspecting the flora of a sun-drenched rear garden. Whilst still sun-drenched, sadly today gone are the rose arches and rockery as the rear garden is laid to gravel and concrete; the house too has also lost its original name. These views were to complement an already large collection of locomotive pictures and cine films built up since boyhood days in London.

The Schneider Trophy air race in September 1929 was also recorded on film by Alistair although sadly the authors have yet to trace any photographic record of the special Terrier-hauled shuttle service between Ryde Pier Head and Esplanade. This was believed to have been pull and push worked whilst all other trains were terminated at Ryde St Johns Road for the duration of the race. Later, in May 1932, Mac with a number of family and friends took a short cruise to Gibraltar on the RMS *Aquitania*, again recorded for posterity by the camera, souvenir items carefully preserved by son Ewan and the whole trip to become a fond family memory in later years.

A.B.MacLeod's films were donated to the National Film Archive and still provide enjoyment to thousands at special showings. His stills photography was spread far and wide, some two hundred plus negatives finding a home in the National Railway Museum; other prints turn up un-credited on occasions and Ian Allan Publishing has a large selection. The Isle of Wight Steam Railway Museum has an increasing collection of photographs and artefacts....and this is just the very tip of the MacLeod iceberg!

Above: Ewan MacLeod and cuddly friend pose in the family Talbot for father's camera outside *Olga House*, at Springvale, Seaview.
(Photo: E.MacLeod collection)

Right: Family snapshot of the garden at *Olga House* taken in the early 1930s.
(Photo: E.MacLeod collection)

Moving model Railway.

Left: A shot from the family album, this was the occasion of the move from Ryde to Springvale. Alistair's caption 'Moving model Railway' probably understates the effort!
(Photo: E.MacLeod collection)

Below: *The Ghost Train* programme from Monday 25th April 1932. (E.MacLeod collection)

PROGRAMME

"THE GHOST TRAIN."
◆ ◆ ◆ ◆ ◆ ◆ ◆ ◆

CHARACTERS
(In order of their appearance) :

Saul Hodgkin (Stationmaster at Fal Vale Station)	Mr. A. E. Antill
Richard Winthrop	Mr. G. H. Johncox
Elsie (his Wife)	Mrs. G. H. Johncox
Charles Murdock	Mr. F. Brewster
Peggy (his Wife)	Miss D. Sutton
Miss Bourne	Mrs. H. Wordsworth
Teddie Deakin	Mr. H. Wordsworth
Julia Price	Mrs. A. E. Antill
Herbert Price	Mr. H. C. Fowler
John Sterling	Mr. E. Searle
Jackson (a Detective)	Mr. A. Kelleway

◆ ◇ ◇ ◇ ◆

The action of the Play takes place in the small general waiting room at Fal Vale, a wayside Station on the South Cornwall Joint Railway during the course of 4 hours.

Act I ... ... 10 p.m.
Act II ... ... 11.30 p.m.
Act III ... ... 12.30 a.m.

Time : The Present.

◦ ◇ ◇ ◆ ◦

THE PLAY PRODUCED BY Mr. H. CHARLEY FOWLER

◦ ◇ ◇◦ ◇ ◦

Overture and Incidental Music by the Theatre Orchestra.

◦ ◇ ◇ ◇ ◦

The Ryde Amateur Players have to acknowledge with thanks the great assistance given by Mr. A. B. McLeod, District Assistant of the Southern Railway in the preparation of the necessary effects.

THE NEXT PRODUCTION
of the Ryde Amateur Players will be at this Theatre on NOVEMBER 21st, when it is proposed to present
"INTERFERENCE"
A PLAY IN THREE ACTS
by Roland Pertwee and Harold Dearden.

The profits of all these Productions are distributed amongst local deserving causes and charities.

Above: Presaging a later trip on the RMS *Aquitania*, she is seen outward bound passing Ryde in 1930. Closer to hand, the period details of Ryde Esplanade station include the early SR running in board and lamp nameplate, an amazing assortment of luggage barrows and a selection of advertisements. Note also the gradient board fixed to the screening just below and to the left of the running in board.   (Photo: A.B.MacLeod)

Above: A sample from MacLeod's photographic collection shows IWCR No.2 being winched ashore at St Helens on 11th July 1909. The tide is out, presumably to allow the barge to ground for stability purposes during the unloading. Not sure what 'Health & Safety' might have to say about the worker sitting on the hauling chain!   (Photo: A.B.MacLeod collection)

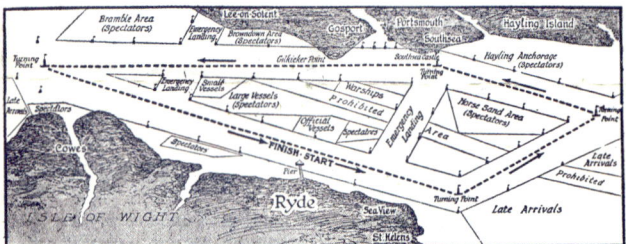

Schneider Seaplane Race
September 7th, 1929.
The Fastest Race in the World
OVER 350 MILES PER HOUR.
RYDE, I. of W.

CHART OF THE COURSE.

Reproduced by kind permission of the "Daily Mail."

— THE —
Starting & Finishing Point is from
Ryde Promenade Pier Head. . .

Adjoining the Judges Box.
FULL VIEW OF THE WHOLE COURSE
WITH THE
SUN BEHIND THE SPECTATORS.

[P.T.O.

MELLISH, PRINTER, RYDE.

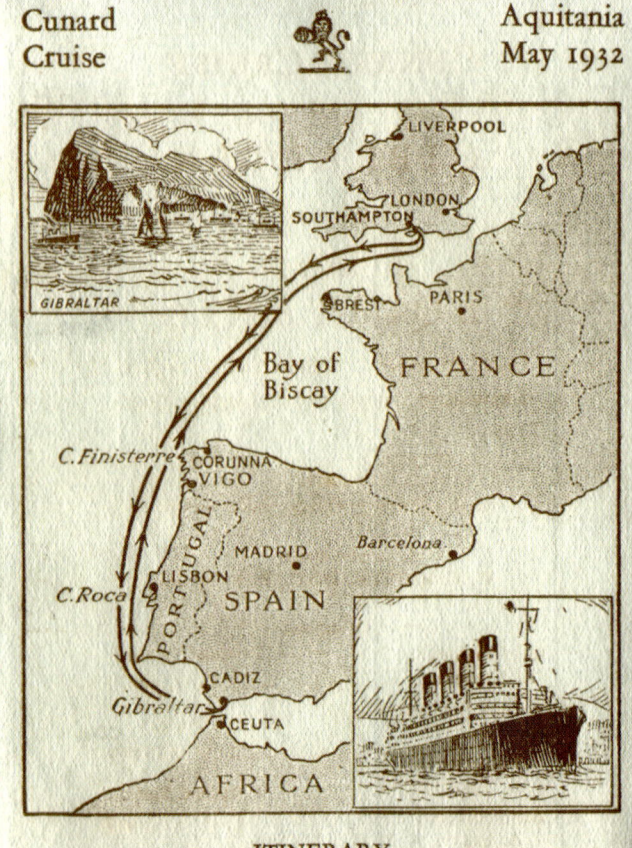

Cunard Cruise   Aquitania May 1932

ITINERARY :
Leave SOUTHAMPTON 5-30 p.m. Sat.   May 21
Due   GIBRALTAR   - 8-00 a.m. Tues.   May 24
Leave GIBRALTAR   - 1-00 p.m. Tues.   May 24
Due   SOUTHAMPTON 5-30 p.m. Thur.   May 26

The itinerary will be carried out, weather and other circumstances permitting, and the Commander of the "AQUITANIA" has the right to effect alterations whenever conditions in his opinion render it necessary, also to decline to accept or retain any person as a member of the cruise at any time.

Top Left: Advertising the 1929 Schneider Trophy Races.
(A.B.MacLeod collection)

Left: The Gibraltar cruise programme.   (E.MacLeod collection)

Above: Alistair tries to look relaxed on 'B' Deck of RMS *Aquitania* during the family trip to Gibraltar in May 1932.
(Photo: E.MacLeod collection)

Chapter Two
To Ryde

Above: Wroxall on 29th September 1923. O2 No.206 heads a down Ventnor train of IWR Metropolitan carriages. The station is as built by the IWR; the passing loop would not be built until the following year. In the background are Castle Road bridge and, beyond, Flux's bacon factory.
(Photo: A.B.MacLeod collection)

In 1920 there were three independent railways in the Isle of Wight. On the east coast the Isle of Wight Railway (IWR) owned lines from Ryde St Johns Road to Ventnor and a short branch from Brading to Bembridge with its important quayside facilities at St Helens. The aptly named Isle of Wight Central Railway (IWCR) operated from a hub at Newport out to Cowes, Ventnor, Sandown via Merstone and to Ryde. In the West Wight the impoverished Freshwater, Yarmouth & Newport Railway (FYNR) optimistically struck out through sparsely populated areas from Newport to Freshwater, until its dying day still vainly hoping for a rail tunnel connection to the mainland. Other than the independent Ryde Pier tramway, a further section of line was owned jointly by the LBSCR and London & South Western Railway (LSWR); this was the double track section from Ryde Pier Head to Ryde St Johns over which the IWR & IWCR had running powers.

In the autumn of 1921 a party of senior officials from the LSWR visited the Island, meeting with the Island companies and offering formal terms for the take-over of the system, no doubt in anticipation of the new legislation about to be enforced. However, this may have been a little premature although one suspects that some planning for the eventual takeover had been made as, when it eventually came a few years later, a couple of suitable locomotives and three sets of bogie carriages

were transferred with almost indecent haste.

The Government scheme to bring about a more efficient national railway system was the 1921 Railways Act. It was to change the situation radically and set out the mechanism to absorb most of Britain's independent railway companies into four main groups. The Isle of Wight lines were to become part of the Southern Railway.

However, there was a certain amount of legal housework required prior to the Grouping and the LSWR was to acquire the Island lines in readiness for the formal handover on 1st January 1923. For both the IWR and IWCR this took place during December 1922, but the ever petulant FYNR took full advantage of arbitration services in the hope of securing a better deal but was finally dragged screaming directly into the Southern Railway in August 1923.

The Southern wasted no time in its plans for the Island. A couple of O2 Class locomotives arrived in May and nine ex-LSWR bogie carriages in July. On 30th August, just four days after the FYNR was absorbed, an exalted team led by General Manager Sir Herbert Walker paid a three-day visit. In the group were A.W.Szlumper, Chief Engineer, along with Edwin Cox, Chief Operating Superintendent; R.E.L. Maunsell, Chief Mechanical Engineer;

Above: An interesting view of Newport North prior to the Grouping. Two IWCR Terriers are engaged in shunting; No.12 is coupled to a Passenger brake van, IWR goods van No.114 and IWR open No.74, whilst the second, unidentified, locomotive is uncoupled. A third Terrier approaches from Cowes. An array of signals is complemented by the 'Beware of Trains' cast notice in the foreground.

(Photo: A.B.MacLeod collection)

Above: A.B.MacLeod's Locomotive Foreman at Newport, Bill Glassey, poses on the footplate of IWCR Terrier No.12 in pre-grouping days. The date is post July 1916, when No.12 was rebuilt as an A1X.

(Photo: A.B.MacLeod collection)

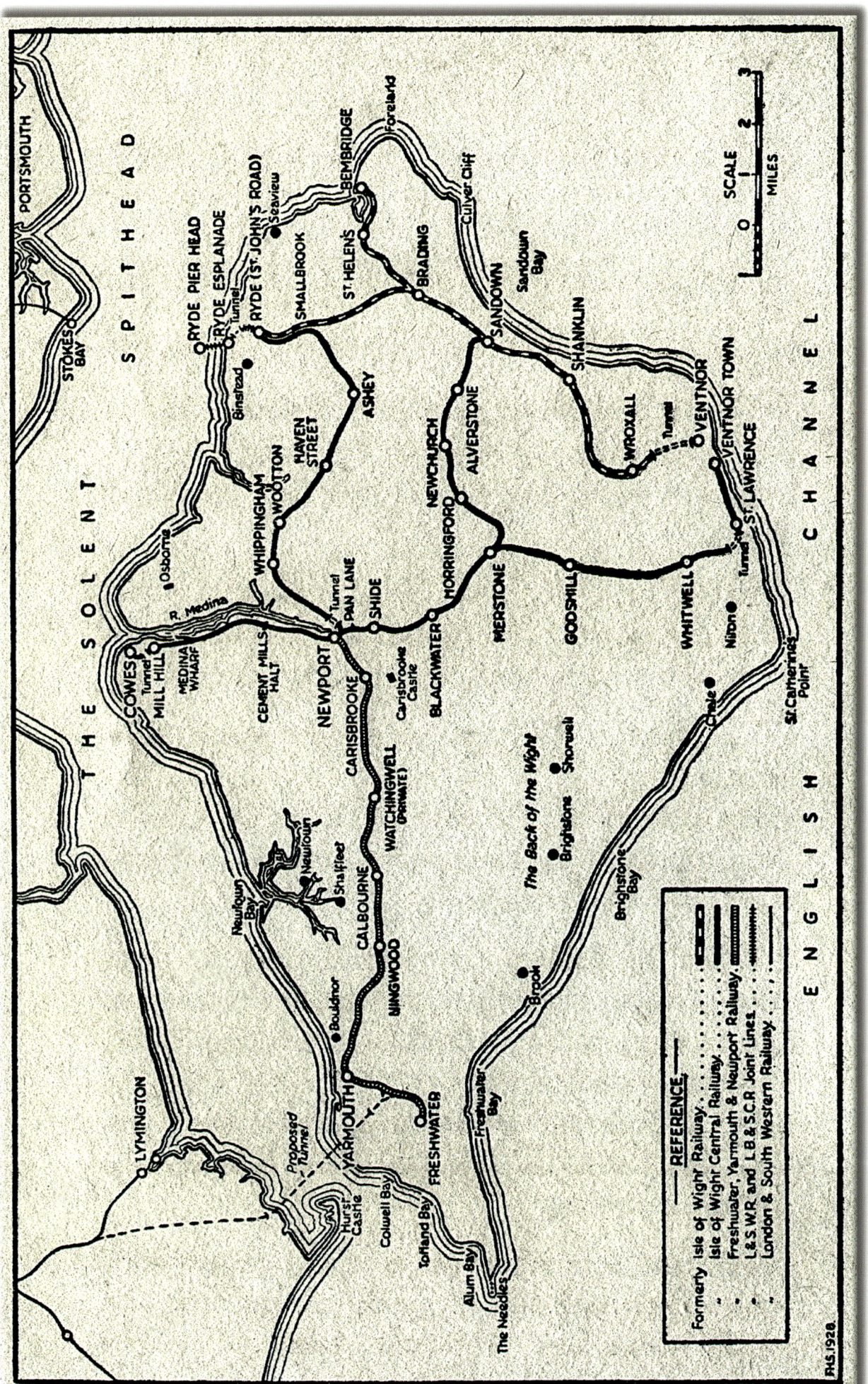

A contemporary map from 1928, originally published in *The Railways of the Isle of Wight* by P.C. Allen.

(T.Hastings collection)

G.S.Szlumper, Docks & Marine Manager, and S.Warner, Carriage & Wagon Assistant. The team inspected every aspect of the operation including ferry services, docks and quays as well as the railway infrastructure. This, the first of an annual inspection programme, set the framework for the redevelopment of the Island's railways.

Many decisions were taken and plans implemented, although some were subsequently modified following later inspections. Key matters included the co-ordination of the Locomotive, Carriage and Wagon shops and Permanent Way departments at Newport and Ryde. There was also to be the transfer of two uniform type tank engines and about ten or twelve carriages, fitted with steam heat, electric light and Westinghouse brakes (the uniform system on the Island) yearly for the next six years. In addition, wagons were to be standardised on a 12-ton variety but a lack of availability resulted in 10-ton wagons becoming adopted. A programme of relaying permanent way, modified track layouts and selected station rebuilding went hand-in-hand with staff rationalisation and a service geared to traffic demands.

Included in the improvements were to be the introduction of pull and push working on the Freshwater to Newport and Merstone to Ventnor branches, as well as a new passing loop at Wroxall. Plans for a cliff tramway linking the town with Ventnor station were dusted off and re-examined.

St Helens and Medina Wharf quays were to be restored or renewed and provision made at Fishbourne for landing motor-car traffic. In an attempt to engender staff pride, monetary prizes for best kept stations, lengths of permanent way and flower and vegetable shows were introduced.

As far as staffing was concerned, locally, Horace Tahourdin, former Engineering & Locomotive Superintendent for the IWR, was retained and made responsible for the whole Island's railway engineering needs, becoming Assistant District Engineer (IW). George Newcombe, from the IWCR, briefly became Acting District Superintendent but soon returned to the mainland, replacing G.S.Szlumper as Docks & Marine Manager. W.J.Sawkins, another IWCR man and former Company Secretary, soon found mainland employment as Assistant Chief Accountant for the Southern.

Such a drastic overhaul of long established operating practices as implemented by the new owners was never going to be easy; 'old hands' Newcombe and Tahourdin were in the front line. There were naturally redundancies and amalgamation of administration and workshops; old rivalries remained and all this was in the shadow of a national recession and imminent pay cuts. Alistair MacLeod later noted that quite a few of the workshop staff had been branded 'Bolsheviks and very difficult'. No doubt if this was the mindset of the previous staff and management it would have certainly led to conflict.

Over the ensuing period a number of managers succeeded

Above: Morton Common bridge, near Sandown 1927. A new span has been built to accommodate the new up-line in connection with the doubling between Brading and Sandown. The two gentlemen posing by the piers are, on the left, Foreman Ganger Brown and, on the right, Chargeman Wilson. The photograph was taken by the Resident Engineer, T.B.Davey. An O2 approaches with a down service consisting of IWR/Metropolitan carriages, whilst a large Southern Railway poster is just visible beneath the bridge. (Photo: A.B.MacLeod collection)

Above: In July 1923 three sets of LSWR bogie carriages were shipped to the Island and allocated to Newport for working services between Cowes and Ryde or Sandown, often with a four-wheel IWCR/GER third as a strengthening vehicle. This is either Set 491 or 492 as it includes one of the Plymouth, Devonport & South Western Junction Railway brake thirds as the third vehicle, recognisable by having no ducket, and is seen being hauled by former IWR 2-4-0T W13 *Ryde* climbing towards Sandown. The date is post June 1924, when *Ryde* was repainted in Southern livery. (Photo: A.B.MacLeod collection)

Above: Yarmouth Quay, c.1930. The fixed quayside crane is handling a Southern Railway B-type container. In the foreground is what appears to be a hand operated diving compressor, whilst behind is the bulk of Yarmouth Castle, built by King Henry VIII as part of the defences of the Solent. Just visible behind the crane is the stern of a paddle steamer berthed at Yarmouth pier. (Photo: A.B.MacLeod)

Newcombe; Horace Tahourdin was far from comfortable with having four masters and retired with health problems in 1926. By 1928, John C.Urie was looking after engineering and Charles A. de Pury was Assistant Divisional Operating Superintendent.

Further decisions taken in subsequent years included a new locomotive running shed at Ryde St Johns Road, the doubling of lines between Brading and Shanklin, the installation of Smallbrook Junction, a passing loop at Haven Street and a fourth platform road as part of a Ryde Pier Head reconstruction.

On the Ryde to Ventnor route Wroxall loop was completed in 1924, Smallbrook Junction in 1926 and the Brading to Sandown doubling in 1927. Haven Street loop and new station building opened in 1926.

In the autumn of 1928 A.B.MacLeod was an assistant to D.Sheppy, Eastern District Loco Running Superintendent, based at Waterloo. Sheppy sent him to A.D.Jones, SR Locomotive Running Superintendent, for evaluation and Jones sketched out the job on the Isle of Wight. Satisfied, Jones sent MacLeod to be interviewed by Herbert Walker. Never one to mince his words, Walker gave Mac his marching orders...he had a new job!

The detail of MacLeod's arrival on the Island is, like the day he first set foot there, a little hazy to say the least. MacLeod suggests he arrived on a wet Friday, took lunch with his predecessor, John C.Urie, who promptly left the Island at the earliest opportunity! This arrival date was supposedly at the behest of Walker who was reputed to have asked MacLeod, *"When can you start?"* to which he replied *"Monday"*. Walker, unimpressed, instructed *"Go over tomorrow!"*

However, all this is at variance to what appears to be a far more professional and ordered approach to the job which was proposed and penned by Mac in a letter to S.Warner, Assistant Mechanical Engineer for Carriage & Wagon. It seems likely that MacLeod had planned to start on 29th October but for whatever reason Urie needed to be away before the 31st and as a result Mac forsook a couple of days leave to meet him, look around and settle into accommodation. A source close to MacLeod suggested he was less than impressed with his predecessor's efforts even though he was the son of the renowned LSWR Locomotive Superintendent!

Whatever the case, when MacLeod was appointed the Island's railway system was already undergoing improvement and a far cry from five years earlier. Within a week MacLeod had explored the system. He had a run in with a fitter who was keeping an owl in the oil store, removed downed telegraph lines from a Terrier chimney and made the acquaintance of a number of characters who were to be pivotal in making things happen.

MacLeod later wrote, *"I knew that when I had got the hang of things I would be very happy here - and so I was."*

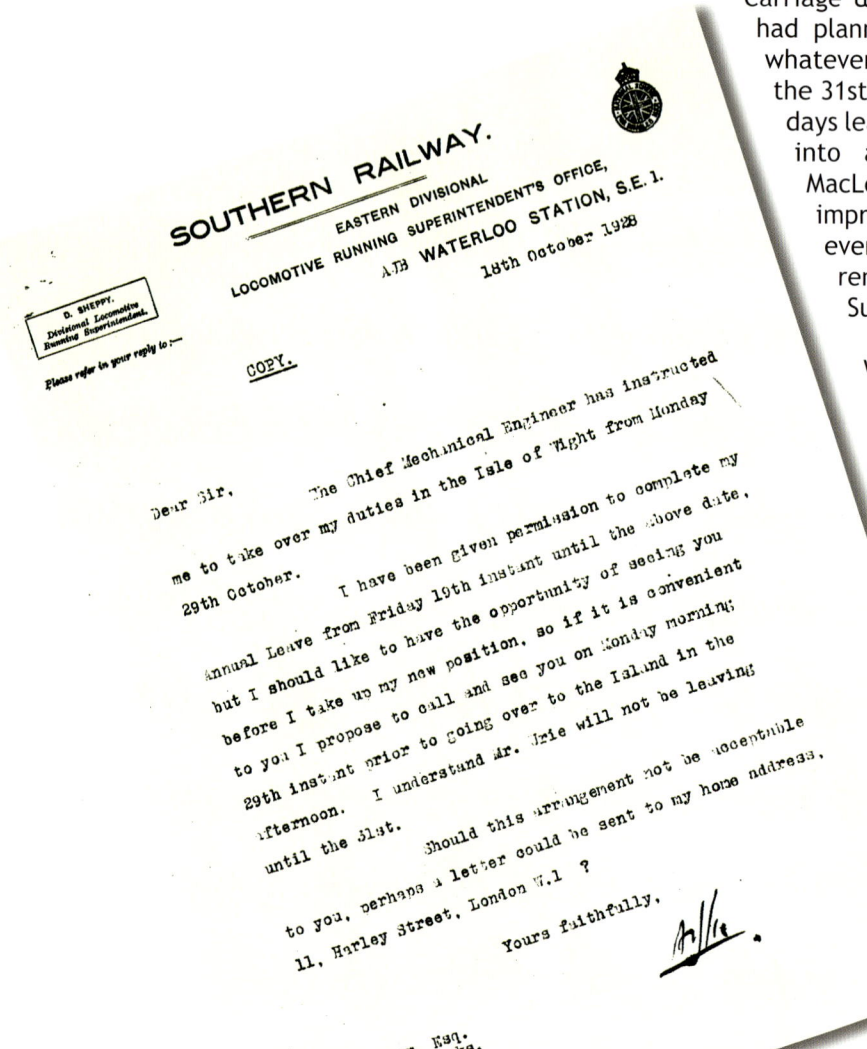

Above: LSWR Class O2 0-4-4T No.211, modified by the addition of Westinghouse brakes but still in full LSWR livery, poses at Eastleigh prior to transfer to the Isle of Wight in May 1923. In August 1924 she became W20. (Photo: A.B.MacLeod collection)

Above: On 9th May 1923, two Class O2s were transferred to the Island utilising Admiralty *Crane Lighter No.2* hired from the Naval Dockyard at Portsmouth and landed at Ryde Pier Head. No.206, later W19, is seen being hoisted ashore. (Photo: A.B.MacLeod collection)

Above: W23 arrives at Ryde Pier Head on 4th August 1925 with a train from Newport. Although not of the highest quality, this photograph illustrates several interesting features. On the locomotive buffer-beam the piping for pull and push equipment may be seen as a horizontal pipe just above and to the right of the coupling, whilst the carriage is the former IWCR Railmotor. Note also the corrugated iron hut and the bell used to indicate arrival of the ferry. (Photo: P.C.Allen)

Above: IWR W18 Bonchurch stands in Newport Yard in 1928, possibly withdrawn. She had been repainted in SR livery in May 1925, with the number squeezed under the nameplate. Also of interest is one of the IWR carriage trucks, 4382, partly visible to the left and the Ryde Pier tramway West electric motor car to the right, both of which had been withdrawn during 1927. (Photo: A.B.MacLeod collection)

Above: The new station building at Haven Street, built following the installation of a passing loop in 1926. At first there was no porch at the signal box door and the waiting room was open-fronted. Access to the platform was through a wicket gate next to the up starting signal and the occupation crossing has been provided with only one gate; coupled with the piles of sleepers, this indicates that work was still in progress.

(Photo: A.B.MacLeod collection)

Above: The track between Brading and Sandown was doubled during the first half of 1927. This is the view southwards from Brading on 5th August 1927; note the timber-decked cattle creep and associated footbridge which led from the down platform to the occupation crossing and unfenced footpath alongside the down line. In the middle distance, Chalk siding lies on the up side.

(Photo: P.C.Allen)

Chapter Three
Staff

Above: A posed view of IWR 2-4-0T W13 *Ryde* near Brading Quay in October or November 1929. Of the gentlemen on the ground, MacLeod is on the right underneath the nameplate and to his right Robert Sweetman, the Ryde locomotive foreman; the other two are probably the Brading Stationmaster and the guard of the train in the sidings. There is also no note of the workers up the telegraph pole. The occasion may have been a running-in turn following W13's overhaul, as a series of photographs, including the LBSCR Billinton set of carriages, were taken by two of the foremost photographers of the day, O.J.Morris and A.G.Ellis. (Photo: A.B.MacLeod collection)

When MacLeod arrived on the Island his predecessor warned him that he would be regarded as an *'Overner'* and therefore viewed with suspicion by the entrenched Island workforce. During his first week's inspection he made the effort to visit all of the workshops and travel all of the lines, meeting as many of the staff as possible. The first impression was that the staff were doing the best they could with the existing, antiquated equipment and, by getting to know them, he gradually gained their confidence. Nowadays, it would be called 'man management'; then it was fostering mutual trust and respect.

The four senior supervisory staff were Robert Sweetman, the locomotive foreman; Albert Brading, carriage and wagon foreman; and Sam Prismall, the head clerk, all at Ryde, whilst at Newport was Scotsman, William Glassey, the locomotive foreman. Finding that none had ever enjoyed the luxury of a weekend off duty, Mac arranged that each would have every third weekend off, as well as regular weekday evenings off, and that he would take his turn at being 'on call' and, to boost their authority, they were told to wear a bowler hat instead of cloth caps. The Ryde men followed his instruction but Glassey could never be persuaded, complaining that a bowler hat hurt his head!

By arranging for improved working conditions, re-arrangement of workshop facilities and taking an interest in the men's welfare, coupled with the upgrading of the system and rolling stock, staff morale was increased. However, some years later, historian and author Alan Blackburn recalled a conversation with Mac at which time whilst agreeing that the men worked under difficult conditions, he added, *"- yes but they needed a kick up the arse regularly!"*

Right: Newport locomotive foreman, Bill Glassey, poses proudly in front of AIX WII *Newport* next to Newport running shed in 1933. As recounted, Glassey eschewed wearing a bowler hat, preferring a cloth cap.

(Photo: A.B.MacLeod)

Above: A fire in the roof of the workshops at Newport being tackled by Fitter Herbert. Unfortunately the date went unrecorded.

(Photo: A.B.MacLeod)

Above: A new cylinder block being unloaded in Ryde Works yard, 1931. The legs of the sheerlegs hardly look strong enough to handle the weight, but presumably they did. The lorry belongs to Shephard Bros. and bears the company's emblem on the bonnet as well as the legend *Agents to the Southern Railway* along the curb rail. A couple of interested bystanders peer over the bridge parapet.   (Photo: A.B.MacLeod)

Above: The ex-FYN Manning Wardle 0-6-0T, newly outshopped from Ryde Works, provides the perfect backdrop for a group of staff early in 1929. On the far left is locomotive foreman Bob Sweetman, but the remainder of the men's names were not recorded.   (Photo: A.B.MacLeod)

Above: The wrecking gang at Newport on 23rd September 1930 prepare to start work on breaking up IWR goods brake van No.2, latterly SR 56033. Having been given SR livery in June 1924, the paint is fading to reveal the old IWR lettering. The significance of the chalked inscription *H.M.S. Whippingham* on the third plank up is unknown!

(Photo: P.C.Allen)

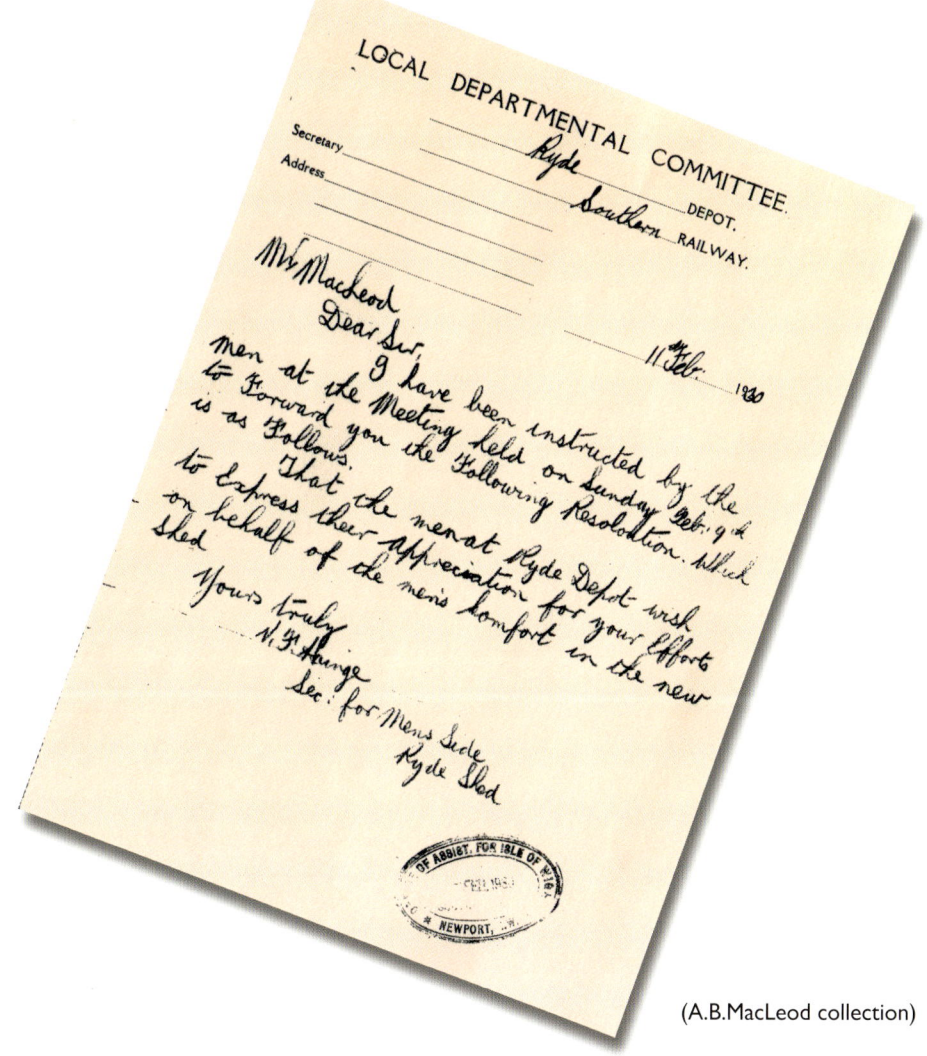

(A.B.MacLeod collection)

Chapter Four
The MacLeod Tenure

An Isle of Wight Appointment.

Commencing as from January 1st, Mr. A. B. MacLeod, the Assistant for the Isle of Wight, has been appointed to control the amalgamated positions of Assistant Divisional Operating Superintendent, Assistant Divisional Commercial Manager, and Local Assistant to the Chief Mechanical Engineer and Locomotive Running Superintendent, with office at Newport.

Mr. MacLeod, who was educated at Cheltenham College entered the L.B. & S.C.Rly service as a pupil under Mr L. B Billinton at Brighton Locomotive Works in May, 1919 In 1923 he was appointed Assistant District Locomotive Superintendent at Brighton, and in 1925 Assistant to Eastern Divisional Locomotive Running Superintendent at Waterloo.

He went to the Isle of Wight as Assistant to the Chief Mechanical Engineer and Locomotive Running Superintendent in November, 1928.

Mr A B MacLeod

From the *Southern Railway Magazine*
(E.MacLeod collection)

It's safe to say that MacLeod was managing the Island's railways at a time when probably they underwent their most important period of investment and regeneration. He was influential in the introduction of numerous local schemes and oversaw major projects. However, we should not lose sight of the fact that the overall plan came from much higher authority - A.B.MacLeod was their man on the ground, responsible for co-ordination and implementation.

In terms of infrastructure, improvements to stations, track relaying and bridge strengthening were still ongoing when Alistair MacLeod was appointed to the Island in 1928 to take charge of the Locomotive, Carriage and Wagon Department. At the beginning of 1930 he was also given control of the Traffic and Commercial Departments and his position retitled *'Assistant for the Isle of Wight'*. He now had input to all decisions regarding the railways on the Island and was able to initiate a number of new projects. These included the following:

- At Newport a new engine pit and ash dump was approved.
- The rebuilding of Ryde Pier Head station, to include a fourth platform road to accommodate increased traffic on the Ventnor route.
- The doubling of the line between Sandown and Shanklin; this continued to be considered but was never undertaken and was finally abandoned with the onset of the Second World War.
- Additional Passengers' Luggage in Advance (PLA) facilities at Sandown, Shanklin and Ventnor.

Meanwhile his influence on other matters, in particular those regarding planning and day-to-day operation, are included in later chapters.

Alistair's son Ewan summarised his father's time on the Island thus: *"He was a 'big' man (intellectually) with great personal skills as well as a commanding presence. Coupled with infectious enthusiasm and a friendly approach, his man-management ability enabled him to obtain the best out of people and 'get things done'. His record indicates that in his early days with the LBSCR and SR he was a 'high flyer' and the Isle of Wight posting resulted from an acknowledgement of his capability, - which was, I feel, a significant element in the development of the Isle of Wight railway during his tenure."*

Ryde Pier Head

Above and Right: An enlargement of part of a postcard, this shows the new buildings at Ryde Pier Head under construction, possibly in 1927. (A.B.MacLeod collection)

Above: Although the locomotive, W23, was the principal subject of this photograph taken on 4th August 1925, in the background it shows a large crane has been erected to assist in the redevelopment of Ryde Pier Head station buildings. (Photo: P.C.Allen)

Above: On 5th August 1927 the new range of buildings at Ryde Pier Head was substantially complete, although yet to be linked to the railway station by a covering of the concourse.

(Photo: P.C.Allen)

Above: Ryde Pier Head station following rebuilding with an addition platform road on the west side, opened in July 1933. O2 W21 awaits departure with a Ventnor train from Platform 1 on the right; set 491 with a LSWR carriage nearest is at Platform 2 and set 493 comprising London, Chatham and Dover Railway (LCDR) bogies is at the new Platform 4 on the left. A new bracket starting signal controls departure from the new platforms. Other features of note are the outside check-rails formed of bullhead rail on its side next to the left-hand road, the ubiquitous bell and a paddle steamer alongside Berth 2.

(Photo: A.B.MacLeod)

Improvements at Sᵗ Johns Road

Right: The old running shed at Ryde Sᵗ Johns was a crude two-road corrugated iron affair and one can imagine the conditions inside. In 1928 an O2 hides within, whilst a workman shovels ash into a barrow on the left. The coaling stage on the right was similarly outdated.   (Photo: A.B.MacLeod collection)

Above: A new running shed was constructed at Ryde Sᵗ Johns during 1929/30, to the west of the station, following the relaying of the running lines. Apart from one man on top of the new facilities block, the others in view appear to be 'knocking off'. The Terminus Hotel is visible to the right background and, beyond it, the frames of the gas holder can also be made out.   (Photo: A.B.MacLeod collection/H.R.Norman)

Above: The new running shed was about as far removed from the one it replaced as was possible. Taken in 1930, soon after opening, the clean, light and airy interior shows the full length pits, washout points, smoke extractor cowling and glazed roof. A locomotive crew stand outside the offices/mess rooms, with various notice boards on the walls. On the original it is possible to read the heading of the large double board as 'Special Notices' and that the time was 4.15pm. The locomotives are, on the left, IWR 2-4-0T W13 *Ryde* and O2 W21 *Sandown*.

(Photo: A.B.MacLeod collection)

Above: Ryde St Johns on 5th August 1927. The rebuilding of the station has yet to begin, although the down starting signal has been replaced with a LSWR pattern bracket, including two elevated shunt signals. Following the opening of Smallbrook Junction, during the summer the down loop on which the train is standing was used by Ventnor line trains, the down main for Newport and the up main by both. In the winter the pre-grouping system prevailed; trains were crossed by the North Box so that the down main became Ventnor line up and the up main reversible Newport. Its signal post has an elevated shunt signal but no main arm. The locomotive taking water is O2 W27, and it is standing over a servicing pit, which was provided on both main running lines. Behind the locomotive is the South Box and beyond it the running shed, whilst backing the up platform is the goods shed.

(Photo: P.C.Allen)

Above: The newly rebuilt station at Ryde St Johns Road in 1930 and a picture with a lot of other interesting details. On the left the new concrete fencing is beginning to be adorned with posters, although not every panel has yet received one. Behind is an LCDR brake third carrying a Ryde/Haven Street/Newport/Cowes destination board, coupled to an LCDR guard/luggage van and the unique 1-compartment IWCR/LSWR brake third SR 4098. At the end of the siding is the IWR/North London Railway (NLR) third converted to tool van 444S. On the down main a Cowes train is headed by an O2 fitted with four coal rails, whilst on the down bay W23 waits with a Ventnor train. The LCDR 2-set, 511, on the right, comprises brake third 4136, unique in retaining a ducket, and composite 6382 with an LSWR Guard/Luggage van beyond. On the extreme right is probably the redoubtable Bob Sweetman in his bowler hat, but is that Mrs. Sweetman on the platform he is hiding from? (Photo: A.B.MacLeod)

Right: As part of the upgrading of facilities at Ryde Works a 25-ton hand-operated hoist was transferred from Bournemouth and erected over No.4 road. Its proximity to the works necessitated locomotives having to have their bunker nearest the buildings for lifting. (Photo: A.B.MacLeod)

Passenger Luggage

Above: The introduction of Passengers' Luggage in Advance (PLA) caused problems with platforms being crowded with luggage. This is Shanklin in 1933 and, in addition to the platform, a rake of LBSCR vans stand in the bay, also in PLA traffic. The carriage is LCDR bogie full brake 1012, formed at the Ryde end of Set 497 instead of a brake third.   (Photo: A.B.MacLeod)

Above: More Passengers' Luggage in Advance being unloaded from LBSCR vans in the bay at Shanklin in 1933. The sheer quantity indicates the necessity for such arrangements, with distribution to hotels being undertaken by carriers' horse-drawn flats. In addition, normal merchandise is stacked at the left, whilst coal is being handled further down the yard. Another LBSCR van is also visible there. Note the coal merchants' hoardings, Jolliffe and T^hos. H.Seed & Co. Ltd.   (Photo: A.B.MacLeod)

Permanent Way

Above: The permanent way gang fettle the track in Brading Quay sidings in 1930. The train consists of a former IWCR brake van, a flat wagon and two ex-IWR opens lettered up for Chief Mechanical Engineer use, so presumably it was locomotive ash that was being used. On the right is the half mile post from Brading. (Photo: A.B.MacLeod)

Above: On the Freshwater road, this is Calbourne viaduct viewed from the west following relaying; the viaduct had been strengthened to allow heavier locomotives although the 15 mph speed limit remained in force until closure. (Photo: A.B.MacLeod)

Left: Ningwood viewed from the overbridge following relaying with bullhead track c1930. The loop was later extended but the platforms were not. (Photo: A.B.MacLeod)

Miscellaneous

Left: Merstone level crossing looking towards Sandown. Public access to the island platform was via wicket gates and board walkways angled to meet at the foot of the ramp. The double track level crossing, the only one on the Island, was worked mechanically from the signal box.
(Photo: A.B.MacLeod)

Right: At Merstone, access to the platform was originally through a subway but, as is evident here, it was prone to flooding and replaced by the arrangement pictured above. The subway remained as a catch pit for water to be pumped up to the water tank, necessitating a bridge to access the signal box.
(Photo: A.B.MacLeod)

Left: At Sandown there was an occupation crossing at the south end of the station, here guarded by newly painted gates. The large notice warned against trespassing on the railway, supplemented by a 'No entrance to station this way' below. A similar notice prohibited entry to the up island platform. The former IWR offices are visible behind the telegraph pole.
(Photo: A.B.MacLeod)

Above: A view into Shide quarry from above the entrance tunnel. Twelve of the Vectis/Blue Circle end-tip wagons await loading. Note the vertical boiler alongside the buildings on the left and the elevated water tower in the background with its high level pipe leading off to the right to supply the steam navvies working at the chalk face.   (Photo: A.B.MacLeod)

Above: In 1929 a new locomotive servicing pit and ash dump were provided at Newport adjacent to the running shed. A rake of close-coupled LBSCR Billinton four-wheelers stand in the carriage siding.   (Photo: A.B.MacLeod)

Marine Matters

Medina Wharf

Above: The new quay at Medina Wharf under construction in 1930. The first of the two coal transporter cranes and its associated hopper has been erected, whilst workmen are busy on the track. Two short lengths of rail on a trolley are visible below the back leg of the transporter.

(Photo: A.B.MacLeod collection/H.R.Norman)

Right: A pair of locomotive driving wheels is being lifted ashore at Medina Wharf using the ex-IWCR six-wheeled Midland Railway crane, whilst the collier *Efos* is being unloaded behind. The rail nearest the quayside is for the transporter crane. The light flash appears on several of Mac's photographs, possibly indicating a pinhole in the bellows of his camera. (Photo: A.B.MacLeod)

Left: The Southampton Docks floating crane is approaching Medina Wharf on 4th July 1932; the load was three E1 0-6-0Ts, Nos.W1-3, five LCDR bogie carriages and three LSWR goods brake vans.
(Photo: A.B.MacLeod)

St Helens

Left: The South Quay at St Helens in 1930, showing four of the six steam cranes which worked there. This quay was principally used for the railway's own materials. (Photo: A.B.MacLeod collection)

Right: The Main Quay, St Helens 1930, with the fixed 10-ton crane and a selection of containers in *Chaplins* and *Curtis* liveries, whilst in the background is the gas works and associated gasholder. In this series of pictures the lack of activity would point to it being a weekend; in fact the only person visible is a lone figure indulging in a little fishing! (Photo: A.B.MacLeod collection)

Left: Bembridge Harbour required constant dredging to maintain the channel to St Helens, which was undertaken by the barge *Ballaster*, utilising a steam crane of the same type as used on South Quay. Two LBSCR vans and a rake of South Eastern and Chatham Railway (SECR) ballast wagons stand on the quayside. (Photo: A.B.MacLeod collection)

Left: Three of *Chaplin's* barges moored at St. Helens North Quay in 1930. The nearest vessel is the small *mv Wilbernia,* outboard of the larger *mv Wild Swan,* whilst almost hidden and alongside the quay is the steam boat *Excelsior.* The North Quay handled general merchandise and its transit shed is behind the barges.   (Photo: A.B.MacLeod collection)

Bembridge

Above: Part of the Southern Railway's estate at Bembridge Harbour was Redwing Quay, where a range of boathouses fronted the harbour. A standard gauge track ran along the edge of the quayside, on which two cranes could be used to lift boats into and out of the water; that nearest is now displayed at the entrance to Havenstreet station car park. Note the large barrels being used as water butts. In the background the Royal Spithead Hotel is just visible; apart from being an hotel, it also saw use as a flying boat air crew base and a school at various times, before succumbing to the wrecking ball in 1989.   (Photo: A.B.MacLeod)

Chapter Five
Locomotives

Above: The end of two of the old Island companies' locomotives in Newport in July 1925. Nearest, IWCR No.4 is partly dismantled, whilst behind IWR W15 *Ventnor*, which had only been repainted in April 1924, has lost her driving wheels and boiler mountings.

(Photo: A.B.MacLeod collection)

The gradual replacement of the old Island locomotives with a standard class for the majority of work began to give a uniformity which made rostering much easier. As the permanent way was relaid and bridges strengthened, the ex-LSWR Class O2 locomotives could be used on almost the entire Island network. The exceptions were the Bembridge branch, where former Island engines and Terriers held sway until the rebuilding of the turntable in 1936 and on the lightly trafficked Ventnor West branch as well as the Shide to Cement Mills cement trains. For these services a small fleet of ex-LBSCR Terriers was maintained. Until late 1931 the Freshwater branch was also restricted to Terriers and two ex-IWR tanks.

The increasing tonnage of coal handled at the rebuilt Medina Wharf demanded a more powerful locomotive which could haul heavier loads amongst the intensive passenger services on the single line between Newport and Cowes. MacLeod suggested ex-LBSCR Class E1 0-6-0 tanks, being almost enlarged versions of the Terriers. Four were transferred, three in 1932 and the fourth in 1933. They were able to handle 40 loaded minerals compared to the smaller engines' limit of 25. These locomotives also found their way on to passenger trains including part of the prestigious *The Tourist* through train

working. However, they were prone to a 'surging' motion which was eventually partly negated by the addition of increased balance weights to the wheels.

In 1928 a policy of naming Island locomotives after local places was initiated, following the example set by the IWR. Quite who suggested this is uncertain. It may well have been part of a broader programme to name locomotives proposed by the Southern's Public Relations Officer, John Elliot. It definitely pre-dates MacLeod's arrival, although the first nameplates were not fitted until October 1928 when Terrier W2 became *Freshwater*. The nameplate was crammed between the 'Southern' and the number on the tankside, in the same style as had been adopted for the ex-IWR locomotives, which gave an overcrowded appearance. For all subsequent namings, the number was moved to the bunker side, probably at MacLeod's behest.

Towards the end of 1931 ex-IWR *Wroxall* had her small cab replaced with that originally fitted to IWCR No.8, kept after she had been scrapped in 1929. To keep within the Island's restricted loading gauge, the four E1's received Drummond pattern chimneys when overhauled at Eastleigh. The five Terriers with 13" or 14" cylinders

6-11-30.

MEMO.

ISLE OF WIGHT ROLLING STOCK.

I have been into this question with Mr. MacLeod, and it is suggested that the withdrawal and replacement of stock for 1931 should be dealt with as follows :-

Locomotives :-

There are 16 O.2 class bogie tanks, and 7 'Terrier' class Locos. on the Island, in addition to the following three old Island engines which are still at work :-

No. W.1 "Medina",	Saddle tank,	0-6-0.
W.13 "Ryde",	Side tank,	2-4-0.
W.16 "Wroxall",	do.	2-4-0.

Particulars of Locomotives are shown on Statement "A" attached.

Mr. MacLeod states these engine are in sufficiently good condition for work until the end of 1931 when the position should be reviewed as to the engines to be condemned, and the engines required to replace them for the Summer of 1932.

It will not, therefore, be necessary for the fourth engine ('Terrier' class) to be sent to the Island for the Summer of 1931.

Passenger Carrying Stock :-

The question of the Coaching Stock has already been considered between Mr. MacLeod, the Traffic Manager's Department, and myself, and I enclose a memo. of a Meeting held at Waterloo on the 2nd of October last in connection with the matter from which you will see it is recommended that the Stroudley,(average age 44 years) and Billinton (average age 34/5 years) four wheeled Brighton stock should be withdrawn from service, and replaced by 15 L.C.D.R. bogies

Particulars of Stroudley 4-wheeled coaches and Billinton 4-wheeled coaches are shown on statements "B" and "C", respectively.

MacLeod has signed and dated the top of this file copy of a memo. Unfortunately it has not been possible to establish with certainty the author nor to whom it was directed. However, it makes interesting reading and gives an indication as to the level of influence MacLeod had on local matters.　　　　(A.B.MacLeod collection)

If the above is agreed, in addition to providing better riding, it will further standardise the stock on the Island as the spares for the 4-wheeled and bogie Chatham stock are interchangeable.

With regard to the old I. of W. stock still on the Island (see Statement "D") the four bogie vehicles are in good condition, and fit for several years further service.

Eleven of the thirteen 4-wheeled vehicles have been finally withdrawn from traffic and are being replaced with the vehicles as shown in Rolling Stock Minute No. 149 dated 31st March, 1930, which have been sent to the Island with the exception of three bogie which will be sent over early in 1931.

Third Brakes Nos. 4098 and 4104 are vehicles specially fitted for the protection of mails, and are in fair condition, and as only Postal Officials travel in them it is suggested they should be transferred to "Other Coaching Stock Vehicles".

<u>Non-Passenger Carrying Vehicles</u> :-

Old I. of W. Section Horse Box No. 3369 has been condemned on condition, and will not be replaced if Ashey Races are discontinued.

<u>Wagon Stock</u> :-

From Statement "E" attached it will be seen that 106 old I. of W. Open wagons are in existence, twenty of which will be withdrawn this year; the remaining 86 will be withdrawn when the 86 agreed are sent to the Island.

The remaining old I. W. vehicles of various classes will be withdrawn with the exception of old Midland Goods Brake No. 56037. Goods Brake No. 56034 needs replacement, together with Goods Brake 56036 transferred to Service Vehicle 445.S., Engineer's Department.

<u>Ballast Wagons</u> :-

There are sixteen 4-ton dumb buffer wagons in existence, sent to the Island for the Brading - Sandown widening. These will be broken up during 1930 - 1931, and will not require replacement.

Two of the 18 Price & Reeves Eastern Section Ballast wagons have been condemned owing to condition, and will require replacement as early as possible.

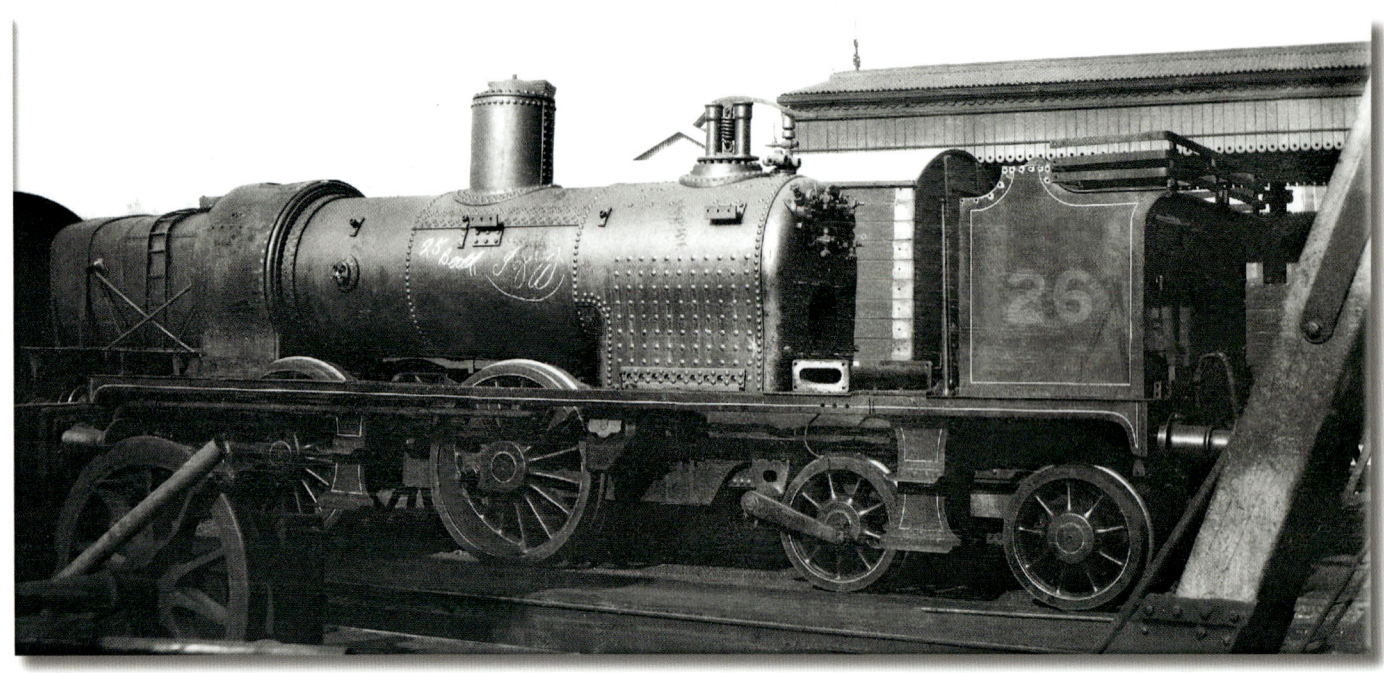

Above: O2 W26 in a decided state of undress! She has received a new boiler, witness the chalked inscriptions '25 Berth' and 'I of W' indicating its transport from Southampton Docks, and is in the middle of a major overhaul. Taken in 1932, W26 would be the first O2 to be fitted with the MacLeod bunker before release to traffic. (Photo: A.B.MacLeod)

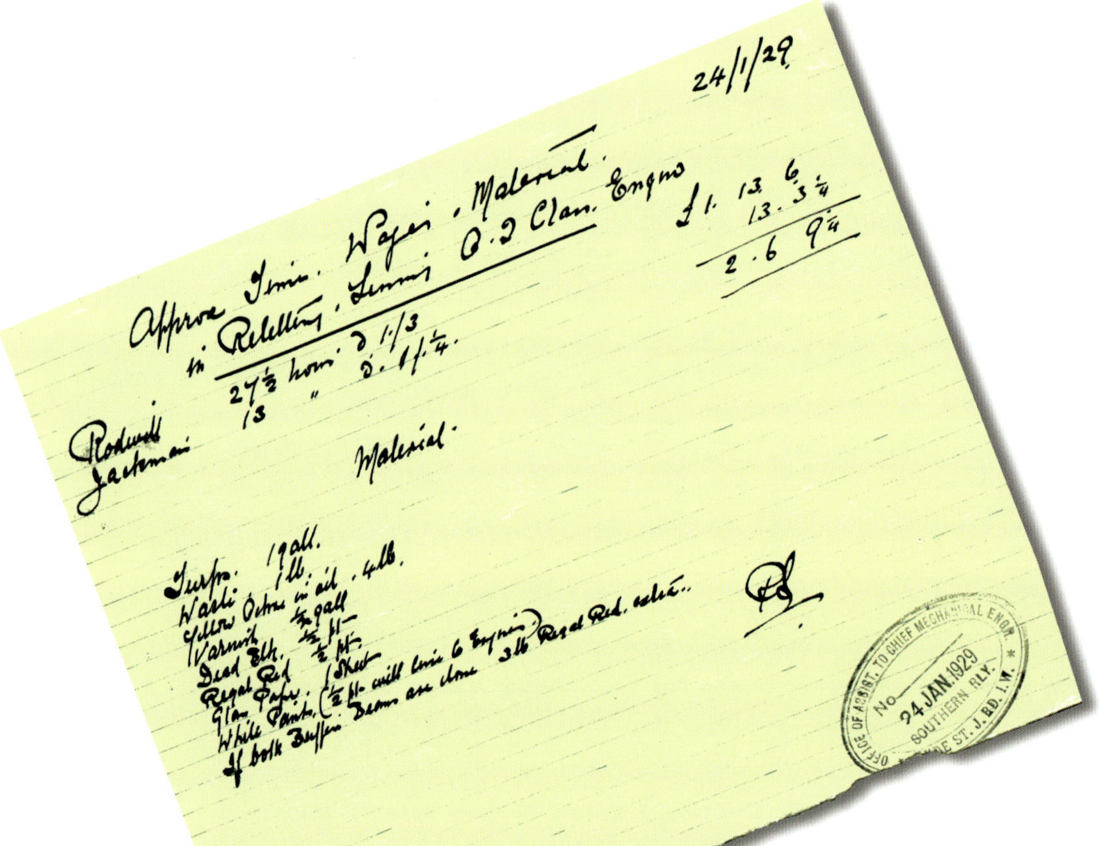

24/1/29

Approx Time. Wages. Material.
in Relettering. Lining O.2 Class Engns

£1. 13. 6
13. 3¾
2. 6 9¾

Rodwell 27½ hours 1/3
Jackman 13 " 1/1¼

Material.

Turps. 1 gall.
Waste 1 lb.
Yellow Ochre in oil. 4 lb.
Varnish ½ gall
Dead Blk. ½ pt
Regal Red ½ pt
Glass Paper 1 Sheet
White Paint. (½ pt will line 6 Engines)
If both Buffers Beams are done 3 lb Regal Red extra.

Above: Handwritten estimate by Bob Sweetman of the time and materials needed to modify the livery of an O2 locomotive, to accommodate the fitting of nameplates and transfer the numerals to the bunker side sheet. Rodwell and Jackman (Jackson) were the painter and his mate. (A.B.MacLeod collection)

also had smaller Drummond chimneys fitted, of the pattern used on the B4 0-4-0T on the mainland. To improve their appearances, the Terriers and the former Island companies locomotives received a smaller 'Southern' on their tank sides, which suited them better. MacLeod regarded the Terriers as falling into three distinct classes; the 13" and 14" engines were the 'Goods Engines,' the 12" were 'Freshwater Line engines' and the 11" the 'Bembridge and Ventnor West Branch engines'.

To engender pride in their engines, individual locomotives were allocated regular crews which, coupled with lining out of wheels, also boosted the standard of cleanliness. MacLeod was keen on this aspect but on one occasion in the 1980s he was on the footplate of W8 at the Isle of Wight Steam Railway in the company of Locomotive Superintendent Len Pullinger. Len's team had worked for hours cleaning the engine and looked for approval from Mac. Surprisingly he turned and proffered a timely warning to preservationists, *"Don't you believe the engines were always this clean in those days!"*, adding that the supposed high standard of cleanliness was a popular misconception.

Left: Seated at his desk in Newport, Alistair MacLeod is clearly contemplating a weighty problem….. possibly the extension to the O2 bunker! (Photo: E.MacLeod collection)

Right: A.B.MacLeod on the footplate of W8 *Freshwater* at the Steam Railway on 14th July 1983. This was the occasion when he suggested to Locomotive Superintendent Len Pullinger that stories of past locomotive cleanliness were much exaggerated. (Photo: E.MacLeod collection)

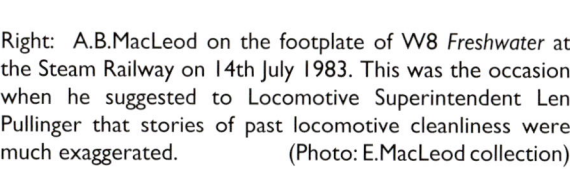

MacLeod's Locomotive Gallery I

On the following pages are some of the pictures that Mac took, or arranged to be taken, of locomotives on the Island.

Above: Here the FYNR Manning Wardle tank as repainted and named W1 *Medina* at Ryde S⸍ Johns in the winter of 1929.

(Photo: A.B.MacLeod)

MacLeod's Locomotive Gallery II

(Photo: A.B.MacLeod collection/O.J.Morris)

Above: O2 W28 *Ashey*, named but with small bunker, stands in Newport loco yard in 1930.

MacLeod's Locomotive Gallery III

Above: IWR W16 *Wroxall*, named and rebuilt with the cab from IWCR W8, stands in the Freshwater bay at Newport in 1931.   (Photo: A.B.MacLeod collection/O.J.Morris)

MacLeod's Locomotive Gallery IV

Above: Terrier No.13 *Carisbrooke*, named and still with the boiler carried when transferred in 1927. Note the copper-capped chimney and the lack of a 'W' prefix. Newport 1932.
(Photo: A.B.MacLeod collection/O.J.Morris)

MacLeod's Locomotive Gallery V

Above: LBSCR E1 0-6-0T No.2 *Yarmouth*, as modified for service on the Isle of Wight, poses at Eastleigh in June 1932 prior to transfer. The coal rails were plated in shortly after arrival on the Island; later cab doors and a second tread to the front footstep were added. (Photo: A.B.MacLeod collection/A.G.Cranstan)

MacLeod's Locomotive Gallery VI

Above: E1 No.4 *Wroxall* beautifully lit by low sun at Newport shortly after transfer in 1933. W4 arrived with its coal rails already plated in and with the power classification letter 'A' painted on the front valance. (Photo: A.B.MacLeod collection/O.J.Morris)

THAT BUNKER

If there is one single thing for which A.B.MacLeod is remembered it has to be the design of the O2 Class locomotive extended bunker. However, this was not a solo project. He was ably assisted in this endeavour by Bob Sweetman, an ex-IWR man and foreman at Ryde works. Mac was always willing to give credit where it was due and rather than retell the story of the bunker, here is the detail from the pen of the man himself, Alistair MacLeod, writing in 1981:

"I remember when planning the Summer train service for 1933 Saturdays, that the question of the number of engines working the Ryde-Ventnor trains was too expensive; and if possible by some means one less engine in steam should suffice.

The trouble was the necessity for light engine running from Ryde Pier Head to Ryde St Johns Road for coal. Changing engines at St John's Road was suggested, but this would upset the tight schedule of Saturday trains.

Bob Sweetman, my works foreman at Ryde works, and I discussed the problem. If only the Ventnor Service engines could avoid having to run light for coaling from the Pier Head, more than once, by carrying more coal in their bunkers; we could save an engine.

We drew out an easy conversion for the three coal rails of the bunkers to be duplicated. However this was thought to add to mess already made in using semi-dust coal. Plates could be put behind the rails, but would look ugly. A high solid-sided bunker was the next suggestion and would be the equivalent of the first idea of six coal rails added to the existing bunker.

VARIATIONS ON THE ORIGINAL O2 BUNKER

Left: As transferred, the first O2s retained the LSWR features of the bunker including six position lamp brackets, and open coal rails, as displayed by No.211, later W20 *Shanklin*.
(Photo: A.B.MacLeod collection)

Below: From 1928, the Island locomotives received names, which required the numerals to be resited on the bunker side. Although still retaining LSWR lamp brackets, discs have replaced lamps, the sides of the coal rails have been plated in and an oval brass number plate fitted. W29 was at Ryde Esplanade in July 1930.   (Photo: P.C.Allen)

Left: W32 was also photographed in July 1930 bearing the same modifications as W29, apart from the LSWR lamp brackets being replaced with SR style lamp irons. Interestingly, the two intermediate irons have also been retained, even though there was no requirement for them on the Island.   (Photo: P.C.Allen)

This was done on W19 Osborne. The engine crews however complained that the view through the rear cab spectacles when running down Ryde Pier in windy weather was so restricted as to be dangerous. I kept thinking about the problem, and when sitting at my desk in my office at Newport, the answer came. R.E.L. Maunsell, the CME of the Southern, who was one of my chiefs, had given me framed signed photographs of the locomotives he had designed for the SR and these were hung on the wall facing my desk.

As I looked at two tank engines he had built, i.e. the Z class 0-8-0T and the W class 2-6-4T, I visualised a bunker for the O2s, bowing out over the rear buffer beam, but coming to the bottom in two gentle curves, and at the same time lowering the top of the bunker to the base level of the rear spectacles.

Sweetman and I drew this out and made a template. We found that the bunker capacity could be doubled, i.e. from 1½ tons to 3 tons of coal, without I think any alteration to the bogie springing.

Work was started on the engine which was then in Ryde Works, one of the Adams boilered series, W26 Whitwell, and the new bunker fitted. This was satisfactory to the

EVOLVING THE DESIGN

Right: Whilst this photograph is slightly out of focus, it depicts an unknown O2 in Newport works having a fourth coal rail and full plating added. Although pictured by ABM, he does not mention this first attempt to improve capacity in any of his writings and only three O2s, W27, 31 and 32, are known to have received this modification.
(Photo: A.B.MacLeod)

Left: The first modified, fully plated bunker was fitted to W19 Osborne in August 1932 and was slightly higher than a fourth coal rail. As detailed in the main text, it was not a success. (Photo: A.B.MacLeod)

Right: The final version of the 'MacLeod' bunker was at the same height as the fourth coal rail experiment, but also extended the back outwards from close above the buffer beam, as shown on W22 Brading at Ryde St Johns.
(Photo: A.B.MacLeod)

drivers and firemen, and thus became the standard bunker for the future for the O2s on the Island. W19 was taken back into the works as soon as possible and a new bunker fitted."

Mac's words perhaps don't contain all the detail and tend to foreshorten the whole procedure. In 1931, Nos. 27, 31 and 32 were fitted with a fourth coal rail. This was followed in August 1932 by No. 19, which received a slightly higher, fully plated extension in place of the rails and which caused the most complaint from crews, particularly when working bunker first...which, lets face it, was half the time!

The introduction of the backward extension immediately above the buffer beam, carried up to the height of the fourth coal rail, enabled the bunker capacity to be more than doubled to 3 ¼ tons but necessitated the packing of

the rear buffers by an inch to provide sufficient clearance. No.26 was the first fitted in September 1932. The Ryde based engines Nos.17-25 were first done, including No.19 which was further altered to the new standard. Newport locos Nos.27-32 followed and subsequent transfers had the large bunker fitted at Eastleigh before arrival on the Island.

By way of a final word on the bunker extensions, it should be noted that Richard Maunsell's leading locomotive draughtsman was William Glynn Hooley and it was he who produced the original Z Class design for him in 1926, and later the Class W. Hooley, in his earlier days with the South Eastern & Chatham Railway (SECR), designed the solitary S Class tank rebuild of a Class C tender locomotive. This unique engine was the first to carry the trademark 'Hooley' bunker extension, thus taking the concept back to 1917.

Below: The first O2 to be fitted with the MacLeod bunker was W26 *Whitwell*, recorded here at Ryde St Johns in the Autumn of 1932.
(Photo: A.B.MacLeod collection/O.J.Morris)

DRAUGHTS

Not all of MacLeod's innovations were as successful as the O2 bunker. Some were short-lived experiments which, whilst great on paper, proved to be of less benefit in traffic.

Complaints about draughts through cabs resulted in the fitting of cab doors to all locomotives during 1932/3 and, in an attempt to improve the lot of crews at Medina Wharf, E1 W2 *Yarmouth* was additionally fitted with a folding screen on the 'weather' side. We let Mac take up the story:

"I fitted all the locomotives in the Island with cab doors for engine crew comfort. Even so the draught from the south-west prevailing wind when shunting at Medina Wharf all day was most noticeable in the E1 cabs. I therefore evolved a side screen which would give greater protection.

The fitting was on one side only and folded back into the cab. The experiment lasted a few months, but it was found that the screen when not in use took up too much room, and it was agreed should be discarded. I suppose the engine crews then brought additional woollies when on that turn. I cannot remember."

Whilst MacLeod was certainly responsible for the fitting of cab doors in the Island, at a recent Isle of Wight Steam Railway Mutual Improvement Class one eagle-eyed attendee spotted a door on the driver's side in an early 1920s picture of IWCR No.11...some ten years before Mac's efforts! However, subsequent searches have failed to reveal evidence of other doors on Central locomotives and it is suspected this may have been a one-off!

Above: The folding door experiment to improve locomotive crew conditions fitted to E1 W2 *Yarmouth*, seen here at Newport, was unsuccessful and soon removed.   (Photo: A.B.MacLeod)

Right: The cab doors fitted to all classes of Island locomotives were fully lined out to match the main livery. This example is fitted to O2 W24 *Calbourne*.   (Photo: A.B.MacLeod)

Below: A slot-in, wooden cab door as fitted to IWCR Terrier No.11 at Newport c.1920. No other Central locomotives have been recorded with such a fitting.   (Photo: A.B.MacLeod collection)

SNOW

Following heavy snowfall in early 1929, ex-IWR *Wroxall* was fitted with brooms akin to besoms and attached to the guard irons; success was limited! A far more ambitious wooden affair was subsequently built and attached to an O2 buffer beam. It was generally felt by loco crews that its very construction was enough to frighten the snow away and it was never used in anger! Details of its final demise appear not to have survived.

Above: In 1929 besom brooms were fitted to the guard irons of ex-IWR W16 *Wroxall* to act as snow brushes. Another of Mac's unsuccessful 'Good Ideas'! (Photo: A.B.MacLeod)

Top Right: Close up of the snow brooms fitted to W16 *Wroxall*. (Photo: A.B.MacLeod)

Right: The magnificent wooden snowplough which frightened the snow away is seen fitted to O2 W18 *Ningwood* at Ryde Shed. Its fitting required the removal of the buffers and the coupling being lifted out of the way. (Photo: A.B.MacLeod)

'MIDGET'

The redoubtable MacLeod/Sweetman team had previously struck when dealing with a tricky problem in Ryde Works, Mac takes up the story:

"At Ryde Works in 1929 periodical shunting of stripped locomotives, wagons and other vehicles was carried out by lighting up an engine especially for this work, which I felt was a very unnecessary expense, and which I was loath to continue. The alternative was to use manually operated pinch bars or special car-shifter bars, which was irksome, slow and caused those employed to ask the work's Foreman Sweetman if some of the staff could come out of the works and push the said vehicles into the positions required.

I suggested to Sweetman why could we not evolve a two man tractor by means of a truck with special gearing and small wheels, coupled together by side rods or chains. As a result we made out some sketches and then visited the local scrap merchant in St Johns Road to see what we could find in the way of bevel gears, sprockets and other cog wheels. This took some time. Eventually an old Ford gearbox became available, and also four small wheels and axles from an IWR platelayers trolley.

So like Topsy the tractor just grew. A wooden chassis and a platform was made to suit the rail wheels and give enough space for two men to stand and turn the handles, which would be connected to a vertical shaft in a column by bevel cog wheels and thence to the gearbox. The gearbox came out of the Ford parts. There would be a ratio 1 to 1 for travelling light, and 4 to 1 for propelling the wagons etc. The connection to the rail wheels would be made by chains and coupling rods on the wheels to stop slipping.

After completion we found that the tractor and two men could move 20 tons of stock slowly and with no great effort, which was better than having to provide a steam locomotive for the job. The name 'Midget' came from my childhood. There was a series of books before World War One known as the 'Golliwog' books, which told of the adventures of Golliwog and four Dutch wooden dolls. I cannot remember their names except the fourth one was an extremely small figure called 'Midget'. I thought this name was eminently suitable for the tractor. The drawings, I have no doubt were scrapped before World War Two. Some of the dimensions were:-

Wheelbase	5' 0"
Coupled Wheels	1' 2" (dia.)
Length (over headstocks)	8' 0" (approx)
Width (" ")	7' 6" (")
Length (over buffers)	10' 0" (")
Weight	1ton 15cwt

The wooden body was painted in wagon brown and black. Headstocks (buffer beams) and buffers were red as well as the coupling rods to the black wheels. The name plates were made of wood with some old gilt shaded black transfer letters on a red ground. The letters SR on either side of the nameplates were cut out of some IWR door transfers of the word FIRST which were gilt shaded in red and white. 'Midget' emerged for shunting in January 1930."

Sadly *Midget* was not as popular with the staff as MacLeod may have liked and became disused shortly after his departure from the Island in 1934. It was broken up four years later, although there was a persistent rumour that some parts had been dumped under the coal stage at Ryde St Johns Road and remained until the late 1960s.

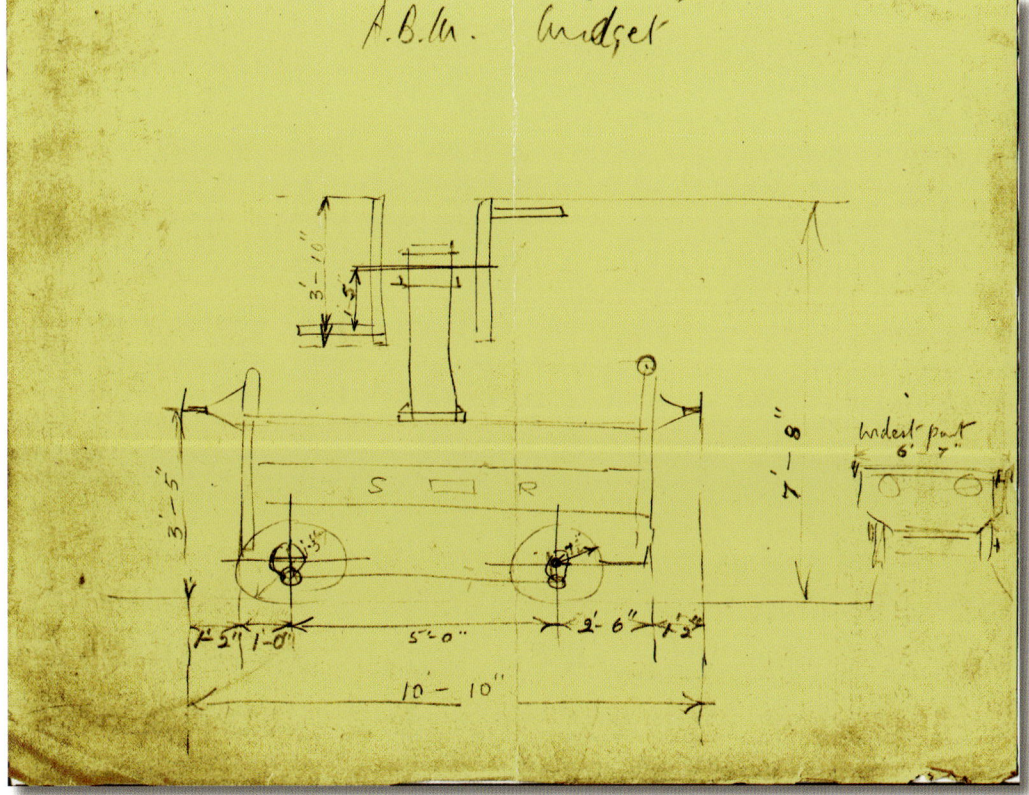

Right: Although the original drawings of *Midget* may not have survived, MacLeod, for some reason, has sketched out the detail on the back of an old envelope although its date of origin eludes us. It is interesting to note the discrepancy in the measurements between MacLeod's written detail and his sketch. Both were from his own hand!

(A.B.MacLeod collection)

Above: MacLeod's 'pièce-de-résistance', the manual shunter *Midget,* poses in Ryde Works yard when new in 1930. Note the former carriage commode handles located on the left hand buffer beam, to assist with boarding the vehicle, which are shown as a bar on MacLeod's sketch. Also of interest is the superb display of posters on the concrete fence panels behind the up platform.   (Photo: A.B.MacLeod)

Below: *Midget* coupled to the boiler truck with two men showing how easy it was to shunt using Mac's pet. Grin and bear it!

(Photo: A.B.MacLeod)

THE CALEDONIAN HOOTERS

William Glassey was recorded by A.B.MacLeod as *"a great character"*; having been for some years a driver on the Caledonian Railway, he then found his way to the Isle of Wight via the Lancashire, Derbyshire & East Coast Railway. As locomotive foreman at Newport with the Isle of Wight Central he was still in post with the Southern when MacLeod arrived.

It was Glassey who started fitting hooters to the locomotives. According to MacLeod's unpublished manuscript *Railways of the Garden Isle*, all of the Central locomotives with the exception of the Terriers already carried them at the start of the Southern era. He further records of the IWR locomotives that:

"The shrill Beyer Peacock whistles were fitted to the 4-coupled engines and, in the earlier days, an additional deep toned bell whistle was also fitted to attract the Guard's attention, when braking assistance was required from the Guard's van, when working goods trains."

These brake whistles were progressively removed early in Southern days.

Following a level crossing collision on the Freshwater branch, an instruction to drivers was issued by MacLeod which required the sounding of whistles at crossings and entry and exit of tunnels. However, it was not long before the shrill whistles caused complaints to come in from lineside residents. MacLeod, another man with Caledonian sympathies, saw the organ-pipe whistle as the answer and extended their fitting to many of the Island locomotives. The mellower note of the hooter ended the complaints and with this another Island railway tradition was born!

Left: IWR W16 *Wroxall* outside the old shed at Ryde St Johns on 4th August 1925, showing the two types of whistle described in the text.
(Photo: P.C.Allen)

Below: W31 was one of three O2s fitted with a fourth coal rail to increase capacity. She also has a Drummond pattern boiler, with the safety valves in the top of the dome. The hooter is also clearly visible.
(Photo: A.B.MacLeod)

W13 'RYDE'

A.B.MacLeod had a particular fondness for the old Island engines and when he came into office two ex- Isle of Wight Railway Beyer Peacock 2-4-0Ts were still in service. Modernisation plans had no place for these antiquities but Mac was determined to see the oldest example, *Ryde*, preserved on the Island. A campaign to save the locomotive started in August 1932 when MacLeod gave an interview with the *Isle of Wight County Press* during which he made the case to keep *Ryde* in the Island rather than let it go for scrap. However, his work did not really allow him to take a leading position and he sought the help of the Railway Correspondence & Travel Society (RCTS) who promptly started a fund to secure the £50 necessary to buy *Ryde*. For a further £25 it would be restored to near original condition with appropriate livery.

By February 1933 about half the purchase price had been raised but *Ryde* was scheduled to return to the mainland for breaking-up along with near sister *Wroxall* and the ex-FYNR saddle tank, *Medina*. Somehow *Ryde* remained, but in January 1934 the preservation attempt was abandoned due to lack of funds. For a few months the loco was superficially restored to Isle of Wight Railway condition but painted in 'photographic' grey. The chimney was changed and MacLeod refitted the builder's and name plates which he had previously purchased. The engine was then photographed from every angle. Quite who funded this work is not clear; certainly not the RCTS and one suspects Mac found a way to make it happen!

Ryde, now stripped of useful spares, returned to the mainland on the floating crane on 13th June 1934, just a few weeks after MacLeod himself had left the Island for a new post. The engine was not broken up immediately but put into dry storage at Eastleigh in the old paint shop, along with a couple of former Island Terriers, two LSWR saddle tanks and the former South Western inspection saloon unit known as *The Bug*. In August 1940 *Ryde* was dragged onto the dump and cut up. *The Bug* was reduced to a chassis and used as a runner in the Works and the body sold. Meanwhile the other stored engines survived the Second World War and were either returned to traffic or found to be a useful source of spares. The South Western saddle tanks had been stored to provide spares and service to the Kent & East Sussex and East Kent Railways, but this was no act of philanthropy as the Southern had a major financial stake in the East Kent Railway and was just looking after its interests! Both locos were broken-up in the late 1940s when they were no longer required.

It has been suggested in some quarters that the stored locomotives at Eastleigh were the start of a collection to be housed in a Southern Railway Museum. Certainly A.B.MacLeod was a great advocate of this and in 1947 said, *"Had there not been a Second World War, I have no doubt that the Southern Railway Museum would have come into being."* Whilst a number of authors have perpetuated museum stories, so far our research has failed to reveal any evidence that the Southern Railway had any such intention. A recent interview with David Allan confirmed that his father Ian, a former Southern Railway employee in the Publicity Department, had also indicated that the 'museum' concept was never on the Southern's agenda to his knowledge but was a popular idea with individuals. MacLeod's best friend Monty Hatchell may well have had a small part in all this as he was Assistant to the Works Manager, Locomotive Works Eastleigh, from 1928 to 1938 and there may possibly have been a private agenda!

What is certain, some managers, not just on the Southern, were wont to tuck interesting items away in discreet corners without official sanction. For this we must be thankful as many such now form an important part of our National Collection.

Above: Two number '13's' at Ryde St Johns Road? Terrier *Carisbrooke* was renumbered 13 in April 1932, and, although *Ryde* is not recorded as withdrawn until July, it had spent time out of use at Newport shed since the end of March. *Ryde* was specially put into traffic on Saturday 2nd July and ran *sans* nameplates, which had already been sent to Eastleigh for affixing to the E1 class locomotive of the same name, which arrived on the Island two days later. This view was almost certainly posed within days or possibly hours of *Ryde's* last trip as it still had fire irons, lamps, and the wheels have a shine.

(Photo: A.B.MacLeod collection)

The Railway Correspondence and Travel Society Appeal

Below: The article from the *Railway Observer* of January 1933. (Courtesy RCTS)

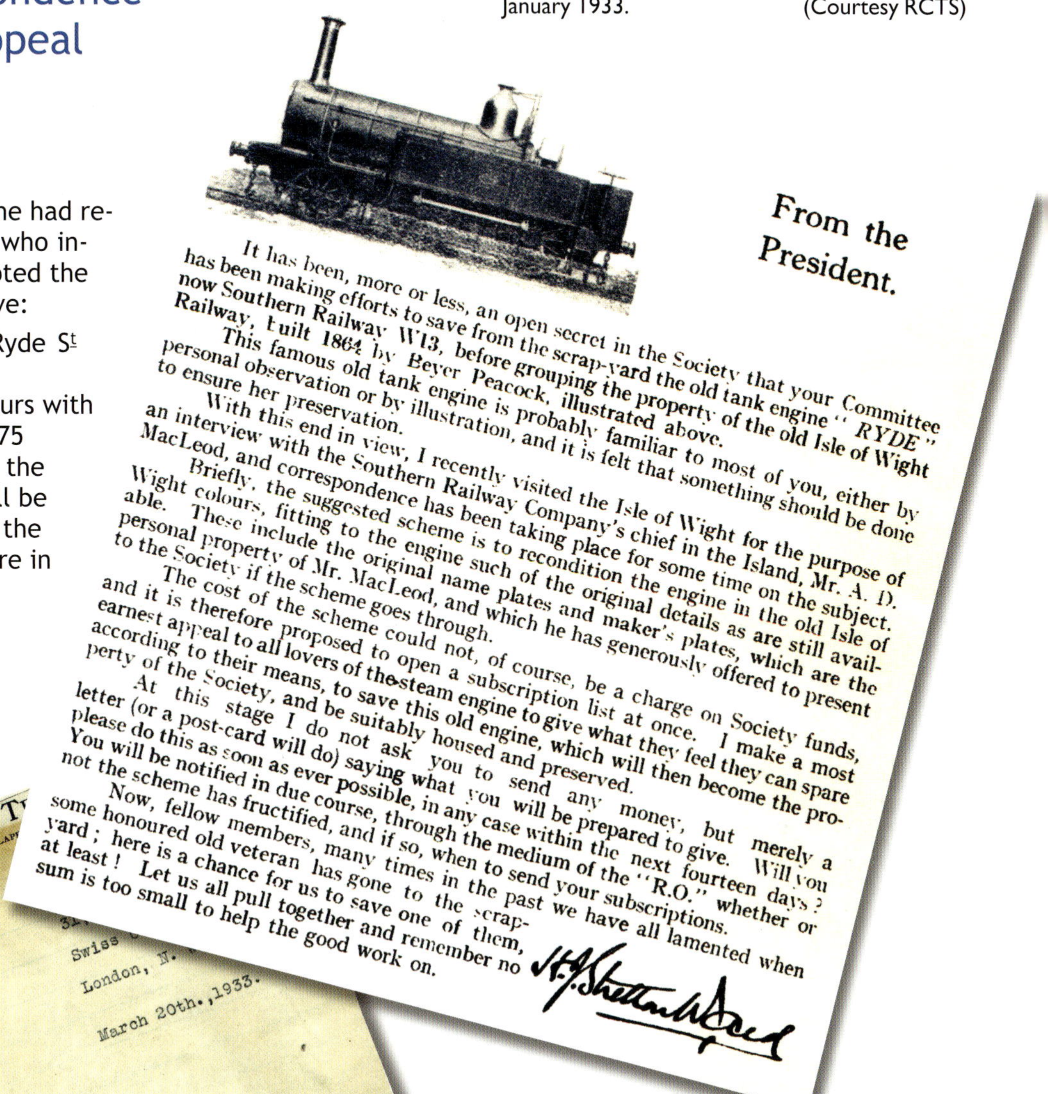

Extract from the RCTS minutes: 29th January 1933

Minute 2a: President stated that he had received a letter from Mr MacLeod who informed him that the CME had quoted the following prices for this locomotive:

(1)   In present condition at Ryde St Johns Road Shed £50

(2)   Repainted in original colours with original fittings at Ryde £75

Mr MacLeod also stated that if the Society purchased this loco he will be pleased to present to the Society the name and maker's plates which are in his possession.

From the President.

It has been, more or less, an open secret in the Society that your Committee has been making efforts to save from the scrap-yard the old tank engine "RYDE" now Southern Railway W13, before grouping the property of the old Isle of Wight Railway, built 1864 by Beyer Peacock, illustrated above.

This famous old tank engine is probably familiar to most of you, either by personal observation or by illustration, and it is felt that something should be done to ensure her preservation.

With this end in view, I recently visited the Isle of Wight for the purpose of an interview with the Southern Railway Company's chief in the Island, Mr. A. D. MacLeod, and correspondence has been taking place for some time on the subject.

Briefly, the suggested scheme is to recondition the engine in the old Isle of Wight colours, fitting to the engine such of the original details as are still available. These include the original name plates and maker's plates, which are the personal property of Mr. MacLeod, and which he has generously offered to present to the Society if the scheme goes through.

The cost of the scheme could not, of course, be a charge on Society funds, and it is therefore proposed to open a subscription list at once. I make a most earnest appeal to all lovers of the steam engine to give what they feel they can spare according to their means, to save this old engine, which will then become the property of the Society, and be suitably housed and preserved.

At this stage I do not ask you to send any money, but merely a letter (or a post-card will do) saying what you will be prepared to give. Will you please do this as soon as ever possible, in any case within the next fourteen days? You will be notified in due course, through the medium of the "R.O." whether or not the scheme has fructified, and if so, when to send your subscriptions.

Now, fellow members, many times in the past we have all lamented when some honoured old veteran has gone to the scrap-yard; here is a chance for us to save one of them, at least! Let us all pull together and remember no sum is too small to help the good work on.

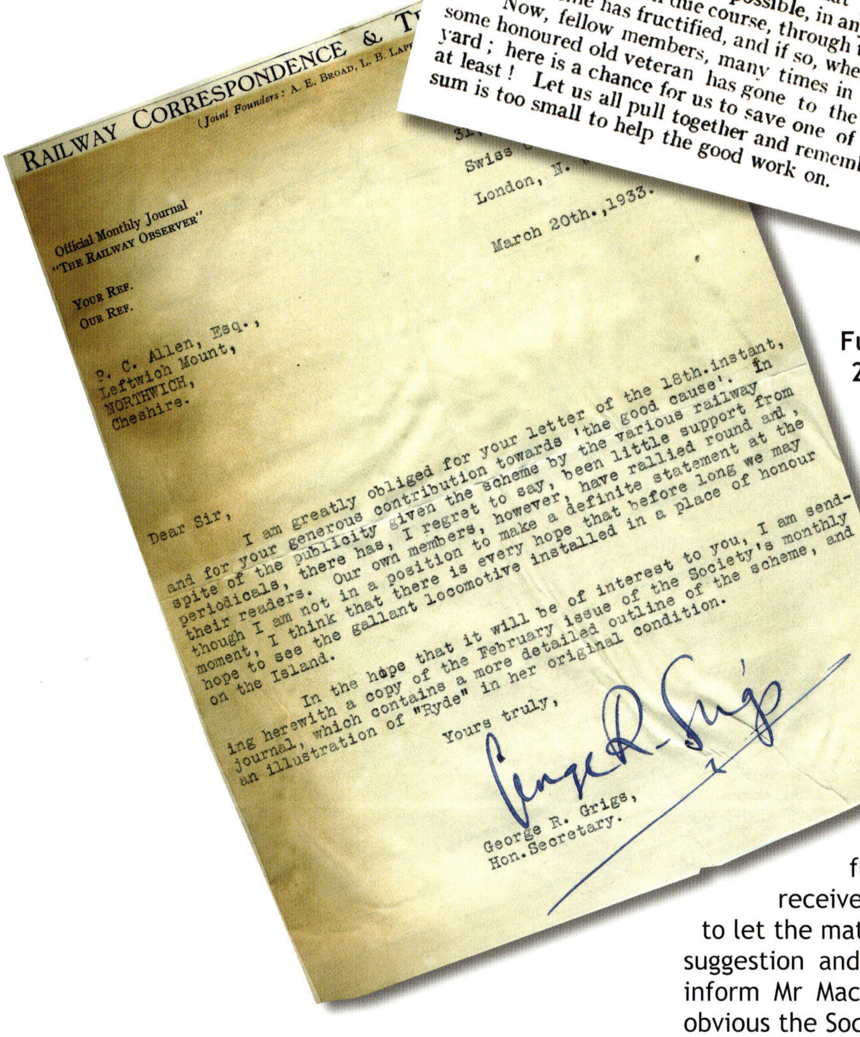

H.J. Shetton Wood

Above: The reply from RCTS Secretary G.Grigs to P.C. Allen's donation towards the preservation of *Ryde* dated March 20th 1933. (P.C.Allen)

RAILWAY CORRESPONDENCE & T[...]

(Joint Founders: A. E. Broad, L. B. Lap[...])

Official Monthly Journal
"THE RAILWAY OBSERVER"

YOUR REF.
OUR REF.

[...]
Swiss [...]
London, N.[...]

March 20th.,1933.

P. C. Allen, Esq.,
Leftwich Mount,
NORTHWICH,
Cheshire.

Dear Sir,

I am greatly obliged for your letter of the 18th.instant, and for your generous contribution towards 'the good cause'. In spite of the publicity given the scheme by the various railway periodicals, there has, I regret to say, been little support from their readers. Our own members, however, have rallied round and though I am not in a position to make a definite statement at the moment, I think that there is every hope that before long we may hope to see the gallant locomotive installed in a place of honour on the Island.

In the hope that it will be of interest to you, I am sending herewith a copy of the February issue of the Society's monthly journal, which contains a more detailed outline of the scheme, and an illustration of "Ryde" in her original condition.

Yours truly,

George R. Grigs

George R. Grigs,
Hon. Secretary.

Further RCTS minutes: 24th January 1934

Minute 3b: President stated that he had now heard from Mr MacLeod asking for the maximum amount the Society could pay for this locomotive. He had replied in suitable terms and stated that the sum in question was £25, also pointed out that some expenditure from this sum would be necessary in order to get the loco to its site. The committee agreed that all sources had been tapped and that we should not get more than the £25 stated.

11th May 1934

Minute 2a: President stated that no further subscriptions or offers had been received, and suggested that it would be advisable to let the matter drop. The committee agreed with this suggestion and it was RESOLVED that the President do inform Mr MacLeod of the Southern Railway, that it is obvious the Society cannot continue in the matter in view of the poor response, and that the best thanks of the Committee be accorded to him for his support in the matter.

Above: Alongside Medina Wharf, W16 *Wroxall* is being loaded onto the floating crane for return to the Mainland. W1 *Medina* is already aboard. W13 *Ryde* was also scheduled for this crossing of the Solent but was held back whilst preservation attempts continued on the Island. 23rd June 1933.

(Photo: A.B.MacLeod collection)

Above: IWR *Ryde* cosmetically restored and repainted in photographic grey, IWR style, in 1933 on the back road at Ryde St Johns. Preservation beckoned, but attempts failed, to eternal regret.

(Photo: A.B.MacLeod)

Chapter Six
Rolling Stock

CARRIAGES

The staged transfer of sets of carriages from the mainland gradually allowed the withdrawal of the old Island companies' stock, although the last of these lingered on until 1931. Apart from the initial transfer of the LSWR bogie sets in 1923, subsequent carriages were four-wheelers, many originally built as six-wheel vehicles. Five four-car sets of LBSCR carriages were the first to arrive, two sets of Stroudley vehicles in 1924 and three of Billinton design in 1925; these were all allocated to Newport.

MacLeod, in later years, told Alan Blackburn that, *"as a Brighton man"* he was ashamed of these vehicles and *"could not understand how they came to be sent."* Subsequently, ex-LCDR carriages appeared in ever increasing numbers until almost one hundred were in service. They, too, were mainly formed as four-car sets, supplemented by a few two-sets, a quantity of loose thirds for strengthening purposes and four full brakes. Allocated to Ryde, their high capacity/low tare weight ratio was ideal for the heavy Ventnor line traffic but they were supplemented by a quantity of LSWR passenger luggage vans to provide sufficient luggage accommodation. Alan Blackburn recalls an interesting

tale regarding these passenger vans, *"Only the 'flat' roofed ones were supposed to have been sent but there were also two or three elliptical roofed ones. The first one of these down the Ventnor line took the valance off the Down platform at Shanklin!"*

In addition there were some ex-LCDR four-wheel and ex-SECR bogie pull and push sets, sent over in 1924 and 1925 respectively. At first the LCDR sets were used in ordinary service as there were no pull and push fitted locomotives available but, following the fitting of this equipment to three Terriers in 1926, they were then used on the Ventnor West branch. When transferred each set was only gangwayed within the set, allowing economies to be made to staffing levels on the Ventnor West line. In 1929 additional gangways were fitted to the inner ends of each set, offset to permit suitable seating arrangements in the first class compartments, but no evidence has been found that they ever worked coupled together. The success of these pull and push carriages seems to have set the scene for the mass transfer of LCDR four-wheelers between 1926 and 1930.

The two SECR pull and push sets planned for use on the Freshwater branch seem not to have been successful and were returned in 1927. The only known photograph shows

Above: In 1933 LSWR four-wheel luggage van 2234 was rebuilt with Guard's facilities and renumbered 1016. It stands in Newport yard fresh from the paint shop in September, complete with white painted tyres, a tribute to the pride of the Island railway staff.　　　(Photo: A.B.MacLeod)

Right: Mac's sketch of the three LSWR bogie 3-sets in 1929, prior to renumbering and rebuilding three of the brake thirds.   (A.B.MacLeod collection)

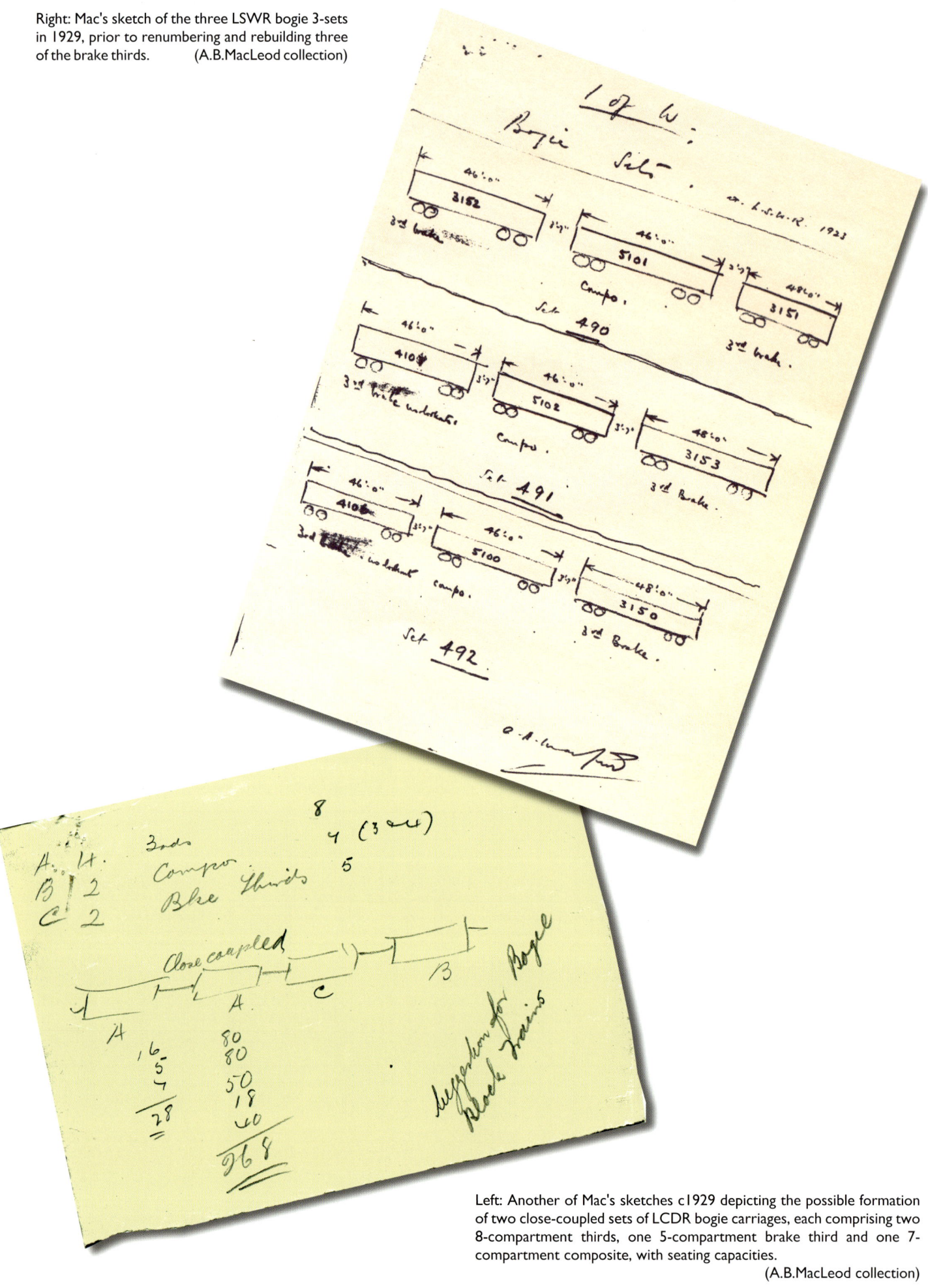

Left: Another of Mac's sketches c1929 depicting the possible formation of two close-coupled sets of LCDR bogie carriages, each comprising two 8-compartment thirds, one 5-compartment brake third and one 7-compartment composite, with seating capacities.

(A.B.MacLeod collection)

Above: Medina Wharf on 17th March 1926 and the arrival on the Southampton Docks floating crane of the first set of ordinary LCDR four-wheel carriages. Being hoisted ashore is brake third 4121 whilst on deck is composite 6374, both part of set 501. The load also included three LSWR passenger brake vans - 1275 is just visible - and O2s W27 and 28. There seem to be many more onlookers than people actually working! This view also shows interesting details of the old wharf and trackwork, but it has not proved possible to read what is written on the large Isle of Wight Central Railway noticeboard. (Photo: A.B.MacLeod collection)

one set in use on the Bembridge branch. Two O2s, one of which was W24, were sent over at the same time, apparently fitted with pull and push pipework, although the equipment was incomplete and seems never to have been made functional. It is believed that the carriages, at 8' 6" wide, gave clearance problems and the O2s could not be used on the services envisaged until the bridges and permanent way could be strengthened.

Returning to the LBSCR and LCDR four-wheel carriages, these proved successful, their fixed formations enabling trains with almost identical seating capacities to be formed according to season. However, in the quest for standardisation the LBSCR vehicles only lasted until 1931 when they were withdrawn at the same time as the last of the old Island companies' stock. Also, by 1930 the supply of LCDR four-wheelers was exhausted and so the bogie equivalents became the next transfers to cope with the increasing traffic demands. Although the running gear was different, the bodywork was virtually identical, so standardisation of spare parts continued. Over the next four years the remaining stock of LCDR bogie carriages all

made their way to the Island. Thus, apart from the LSWR bogie sets and a few 'oddities', the stock was generally homogenous.

MacLeod drafted several permutations of carriages to achieve sets with almost identical seating capacities and almost all the bogie stock was transferred to the Ryde to Ventnor line. Three of the LSWR brake thirds were rebuilt with two additional third class compartments, achieved by removing much of the guard/luggage area. Meanwhile the composites had a former first class compartment, which had been downgraded to third class on transfer in 1923, reinstated as first class. Thus each three-car set now provided seating for 24 first and 150 third class passengers. Two of the sets each received one of the first LCDR bogie third carriages transferred in 1930.

For summer 1931 each set was augmented by the addition of two thirds and one composite carriages, which increased the capacities to 48 first and 270 third class seats. To provide sufficient bogie carriages for the Ventnor line traffic two further sets were formed. One

Above: LCDR brake third 4133 at Ryde St Johns in April 1934 as rebuilt with extended luggage accommodation for use on mail trains.

(Photo: A.B.MacLeod)

consisted exclusively of LCDR bogie carriages, seating 48 first and 260 third class passengers. The other was a real hotch-potch, made up of the two ex-IWCR Lancaster bogie carriages, the ex-IWCR ex-Midland Railway brake composite, and three LCDR bogie third carriages, giving a seating capacity for 36 first and no fewer than 340 third class passengers. The latter set was disbanded after the summer of 1933; the ex-MR carriage gained an extra third class compartment at the expense of luggage space, whilst the Lancaster bogies were rebuilt for use on the Bembridge branch.

Prior to Southern Railway days a variety of rebuilds had been undertaken on the LCDR four-wheel carriages with some third class carriages being converted to brake thirds by the addition of a guard's/luggage compartment, while other brake third carriages had their guard's/luggage compartments removed to make them thirds. In addition the Southern modified some full first carriages to composites for Isle of Wight service by downgrading one or two compartments to third class.

It is perhaps surprising then that MacLeod found it necessary to further modify some of the brake thirds. During 1932/3, brake thirds Nos. 4119/48/50 each lost one compartment to enlarge the luggage area, whilst during the winter of 1933/4 Nos. 4124/33 each lost two compartments; the latter two were for use on the Freshwater mail trains, replacing the last two Island company four-wheel carriages. In 1937 No.4150 was further reduced to two compartment configuration.

MacLeod might be considered something of a *preservationist* in rebuilding the non-standard carriages for extended service when spares were probably becoming difficult to source, although his principal achievement has to be the rebuild of the former IWCR rail motor carriage in 1932/3. The interior was completely remodelled, the guard's compartment being reduced in size by incorporating the luggage section into passenger accommodation and the wooden slatted seats replaced with upholstered ones. In 1934 it was again in the works, when the wooden panelled exterior was completely covered with plain steel sheet. As rebuilt it was used in *The Tourist Through Train* between Ventnor and Freshwater.

One other carriage which was transferred, and which presaged the next type chosen for Island service, was a bogie LBSCR saloon. This was a direct replacement for a four-wheel LBSCR vehicle used for Inspection purposes and which had incurred the displeasure of the Chief Operating Officer during a trip from Yarmouth to Ryde when attempts to serve tea had ended in disaster because of its rough riding. MacLeod visited the mainland to seek a replacement and found a 1916-built former invalid saloon which had been rebuilt as a first class saloon carriage in 1925. It was further rebuilt as a brake composite for use on the Island, and could be employed in ordinary service trains when not required for inspections; as such it was also used in *The Tourist*.

Having exhausted the supply of LCDR bogie carriages, further imports were now LBSCR vehicles which, although longer at 54 feet, would fit the Island's restricted loading gauge, and four brake thirds arrived in June 1934 along with the bogie saloon. The four brakes were allocated to Newport and were specifically rostered on the Sandown - Cowes line where their copious van space was used to good effect on the heavy milk traffic. Although MacLeod was instrumental in their transfer, their arrival coincided with his departure from the Island so he never saw them used actively. He had, however, planned which sets they would be used in, as their increased length required careful diagramming to ensure that sets could be accommodated within existing platform lengths.

Above: The former IWCR railmotor carriage, brake third 4103, was extensively rebuilt at Ryde and the luggage area incorporated into additional passenger accommodation. Although still boasting a 'Ryde & Ventnor' board, its future use was in *The Tourist* through train. The two different wheel-base bogies are noticeable, that at the left, the former driving end, being the original. (Photo: A.B.MacLeod)

Above: When 4103 was steel sheeted in 1934, a single door replaced the double doors to the Guard's compartment. Unusually, it was shunted outside during conversion. (Photo: A.B.MacLeod)

Above: Newly outshopped at Newport in April 1934 is Set 501, comprising the IWCR Lancaster bogies altered for service on the Bembridge branch. The brake composite was downgraded to brake third, losing its duckets in the process, whilst the composite had a former first class compartment reinstated as such. The high quality of the work and paint finish is very evident. The left hand vehicle is LCDR brake third 4133, newly converted to two compartments. (Photo: A.B.MacLeod)

Above: The LBSCR invalid saloon as transferred to the Island stands in Newport yard in 1934, complete with *The Tourist Through Train* board.
(Photo: A.B.MacLeod)

Above: An LSWR brake third freshly ex-shops in July 1931 and renumbered 4140. This example retained its large luggage space.
(Photo: A.B.MacLeod)

Above: Sister LSWR brake third 4139, with two additional compartments replacing the luggage area, also at Ryde St Johns in July 1931.
(Photo: A.B.MacLeod)

Above: The IWCR/MR brake composite 6988 at Ryde St Johns c1932 when formed at the Ventnor end of Set 494. Both side destination and cantrail 'Ryde & Ventnor' boards are carried. (Photo: A.B.MacLeod collection/O.J.Morris)

Above: In 1933/4 an extra third class compartment, which was somewhat narrower than the original ones, replaced the luggage area. (Photo: A.B.MacLeod)

Above: A1X W11 prepares to set off to Freshwater, having reversed out of Newport station. It is summer 1932 and newly transferred LCDR bogie set 495 has been strengthened with two LCDR four-wheel thirds. It is possible this is one of the first workings of the *East-West Through Train*.
(Photo: A.B.MacLeod)

Above: Summer 1934 and *The Tourist* awaits departure from Freshwater behind O2 W28 Ashey. The LCDR bogie set is now supplemented with the LBSCR saloon and the IWCR Railmotor carriages.
(Photo: A.B.MacLeod)

Left: Although seen elsewhere, this is the only known view of the interior of the new carriage paint shop at Newport. Finishing touches are being applied to composite 6384 of LSWR Set 492, whilst brake third 4138 positively gleams.

(Photo: A.B.MacLeod)

WAGONS

By 1930 the majority of the old Island companies' goods stock had been replaced with transfers from the mainland, principally ex-LBSCR open and covered wagons and ex-LSWR goods brake 'road' vans. Following complaints of passengers' luggage being tainted with the smell of fish - there was a healthy trade in the carriage of fresh fish by passenger train - MacLeod arranged for a number of ex-LBSCR vans to be specially lettered 'For Fish Traffic Only'.

Likewise, the introduction of PLA, whereby visitors were encouraged to forward their luggage prior to travel to and from the Island, saw the requirement for special parcels trains; demand for stock exceeded the supply of passenger vans. Therefore, some Westinghouse brake fitted ex-LBSCR vans had brackets added to carry small boards denoting their use in this traffic. They also appear in photographs to have had their roofs painted white; when not required for PLA traffic they were kept together and stored in a convenient siding.

An ongoing need for wagons to carry locomotive ash from the two Motive Power Depots saw MacLeod select a number of ex-IWR 12-ton opens. These were given special lettering and allocated to either Ryde or Newport. Another use for old wagons was in the provision of a new coal stacking stage at Newport. A quantity of ex-IWR opens had their running gear, sides and ends removed before being grounded to provide a level area at a suitable height for coaling locomotives.

The arrival of the more powerful ex-LBSCR E1 0-6-0 tanks enabled MacLeod to increase the length of coal trains between Medina Wharf and Newport from 25 to 40 loaded wagons, thus helping free paths on the single line section for additional passenger workings. To assist with working these heavier trains, four ex-LSWR brake vans were rebuilt with a second balcony and fitted with sanding gear. They were also given Westinghouse through pipes, possibly for working mixed trains on the Freshwater branch. Upon completion of the first of these vans Mac was reputed to have instructed the staff who had worked on it to go for a ride in it!

Above: Although a new, covered coaling stage was provided at Newport in 1932, an extended coal stacking area was added utilising old IWR wagon underframes, stripped of running, buffing and drawgear. The nearest frame appears to be from an ex-LCDR four-wheel carriage. Later, the stack was further extended using additional wagon underframes. (Photo: A.B.MacLeod)

Above: Ex-LBSCR, Westinghouse-braked van 46966, allocated to PLA, as indicated by the small board carried on the upper right of the side. (Photo: A.B.MacLeod)

Right: Detail of one of the boards carried by ex-LBSCR vans in PLA traffic. (Photo: A.B.MacLeod)

Two ex-LBSCR 5-plank open wagons were rebuilt on the mainland as 7-plank mineral wagons, and one was transferred to the Island in 1934. It is unclear whether this was with a view to further conversions, but in the event it remained a sole example and it was not until 1948 that higher open wagons were sent across in the form of SR-built 8-plank opens.

Ever the innovator, in 1932 MacLeod created one of Britain's first weed-killing trains by utilising the two ex-IWCR water tanks, which had become redundant following the rebuilding of Medina Wharf and the withdrawal of the old steam cranes, and an ex-IWR Goods brake van. The two tanks were placed on old IWR underframes and the whole ensemble painted red oxide and lettered appropriately.

Previously, he had taken a withdrawn IWR carriage truck, cut a well into the floor and created a boiler truck for carrying boilers between Ryde Works and St Helens for transfer to and from the mainland. Another rebuild which MacLeod undertook was the old Midland Railway Goods brake van inherited from the IWCR, which had a single balcony and an open platform at the opposite end. He had a second, enclosed balcony built over the open end.

All these various modifications and rebuilds were undertaken in addition to the routine maintenance. Mac certainly kept his C&W workshop staff busy which at a time of high unemployment and general recession was no mean feat.

One cannot end this section without mention of another little 'Mac foible'. When former IWR flat No.1 was withdrawn from traffic in 1931 and transferred to a works wagon at Ryde, he had the east side (away from general public gaze) repainted in IWR livery and number.

Above: The forty wagon coal train trial in 1933, hauled by E1 W4 *Wroxall,* waiting to leave Medina Wharf. The fourth wagon is the unique rebuilt ex-LBSCR 7-plank open, 27545.

(Photo: A.B.MacLeod)

Above: Ex-LBSCR covered van 46945 with the first style of branding for fish traffic.   (Photo: A.B.MacLeod)

Above: A complete repaint for ex-LBSCR 46946 saw a prominent branding for vans reserved for fish traffic. (Photo: A.B.MacLeod)

Above: A number of ex-IWR 12-ton open wagons were specially lettered for use by the CME & Loco Running Department, and were inscribed with an allocation to either Newport or Ryde - really rather unnecessary on a closed system like the Island. (Photo: A.B.MacLeod)

Left: Details of the lettering applied to open 64393, including the italicised 'To be Returned to Ryde Works When Empty'. (Photo: A.B.MacLeod)

Above: The Island's C&W staff undertook many conversions to rolling stock. In 1929 former IWCR passenger luggage van 17 has been converted to a Tool Van for the CME Department at Newport and renumbered 427S. (Photo: A.B.MacLeod collection/H.R.Norman)

Above: Three goods brake vans at Newport c.1932. From the right: ex-LSWR 56054 as built, ex-IWCR/MR 56037 rebuilt with enclosed balcony over open end, ex-LSWR 56048 rebuilt with a second balcony and sanding gear and Westinghouse pipe. (Photo: A.B.MacLeod)

Above: Ex-LSWR goods brake van 56047 as rebuilt with a second balcony and sanding gear at Ryde St Johns, June 1933. Were these two of the men instructed by A.B.MacLeod to *"go for a ride"*?

(Photo: A.B.MacLeod)

Above and Right: The unique, on the Island, ex-LBSCR 10-ton open rebuilt with two additional planks stands on the quay at St Helens in early 1934. The chalk inscriptions read 'I of W Sunday/26 Berth/no Ball'; presumably instructions that it was to be shipped to the Isle of Wight on Sunday from 26 Berth, Southampton Docks and that it had no ballast.

(Photos: A.B.MacLeod)

Above: The underframe of one of the carriages supplied by Oldbury to the IWR, having been converted to a carriage truck c.1920, was modified as a boiler wagon in June 1930 at Ryde Works and numbered 439S. Still unlettered in this picture, it is carrying the A1 boiler from IWCR Terrier W10, which had been rebuilt as an A1X in April of that year.   (Photo: A.B.MacLeod)

Above: MacLeod introduced a weed killing train to the Island in August 1932 by mounting the two former IWCR water tanks on ex-IWR underframes and adapting an ex-IWR goods brake van. The tanks were renumbered 428S and 443S, whilst the brake van was numbered 472S and lettered 'For use with weed killing plant only'.   (Photo: A.B.MacLeod)

Above: Mac's foible! The ex-IWR flat wagon repainted in IWR livery in December 1932. Although only one side was done, that normally away from public gaze, this view was taken in the up yard.

(Photo: A.B.MacLeod)

Above: The IWCR, ex-MR, goods brake van rebuilt with a second balcony. Such was the skill of the C&W workshop in matching the original that it is difficult to determine which is the new work. The date on the solebar reads 6-33 and no tare weight has yet been painted.

(Photo: A.B.MacLeod)

Above: By way of contrast, the MR goods brake van still in IWCR livery at Newport and showing the open platform end.
(Photo: A.B.MacLeod collection)

Above: A busy scene at Ryde St Johns in 1930. Three O2s are in view; W20 *Shanklin* is on the up line shunting, including the two IWR tar tanks and an IWCR/MR van, whilst two unidentified locomotives head down passenger trains. A Ventnor service stands on the down main and one for Cowes has the road from the loop, both formed of LCDR four-wheel stock. Smallbrook box is open as there are only two arms on the gantry. The signal box still has its steps at the south end and one of the elliptical roof LSWR passenger brake vans is in the works siding.
(Photo: A.B.MacLeod)

Chapter Seven
Train Services

Above: In 1933 *The Tourist* began running from Ventnor. Headed by an E1 tank, the formation is LCDR bogie 4-set 495, with 4103, the former IWCR Railmotor, included as the penultimate carriage.

(Photo: A.B.MacLeod)

Traffic had been increasing ever since the Southern Railway came into existence. The 1929 summer season was so successful that the two trains an hour service on the Ryde to Ventnor line was inadequate to cater for the increase in passengers. For the 1930 summer a new timetable of three trains per hour was devised. MacLeod told Alan Blackburn that he worked out the details for engine and platform workings for Ryde Pier on his large model railway and whilst we suspect that it was later more scientifically proved, it is a good story!

Additional coaching stock was needed and the first of the LCDR bogie carriages were sent over to augment the LSWR bogie sets. Traffic continued to increase, such that for summer 1933 a further revision of the timetable was made. There was now an additional 'short' working from Ryde to Sandown which, with the hourly trains to Newport and Cowes, gave five workings in each direction hourly between Ryde Pier Head and Smallbrook. This was later increased to six. On the Ventnor road some services ran non-stop between Ryde Pier Head and either Sandown or Shanklin.

1932 had seen the introduction of a limited stop, through train between Shanklin and Freshwater branded as the *East-West Through Train*. In 1933 it was altered to start and finish at Ventnor and given the name *The Tourist*. Other through workings were also introduced between Ryde Pier Head and Freshwater, whilst Cowes-Newport workings alternately served Ryde or Sandown.

Delays were being caused on summer weekends because of tight timings between the arrival and departure of the ferries and trains. Passenger hand baggage took time to manhandle down narrow ships' gangways; other baggage was bulk loaded into wheeled cages which were craned into the hold and upon arrival lifted onto the pier and hauled to the appropriate waiting train, hand sorted roughly by destination, and placed in the guard's van. To help alleviate the problem, MacLeod arranged for PLA to be introduced to the Island in 1932 and special PLA trains were run in addition to the timetabled fish and parcels trains.

Whilst goods traffic could never remotely match the intensity of passenger workings, there was still a need to ensure that coal imported through Medina Wharf was distributed to the various coal factors and the locomotive depots at Newport and Ryde St Johns Road, as well as the general merchandise through St Helens Quay. On the export side, in addition to milk and seasonally grown fresh fruit, an increasing crop was sugar-beet; mostly grown in the Arreton valley, this totalled some 3000 tons in 1932. It was carried in wagon loads to Medina Wharf where it was estimated the new conveyers lifted about 50 tons per hour into ships' holds.

It was certainly the heyday of Island train working, mostly over single track routes, and called for a high degree of skill on the part of all staff to ensure everything ran to time.

Above: Carriage No.4103 at Freshwater in 1934 formed into *The Tourist*. This is the only known photograph of an Isle of Wight carriage in Maunsell livery with the company name carried at waist level and may well have been the only one so treated. The LBSCR saloon is coupled to it but is lettered in the conventional way. (Photo: A.B.MacLeod)

Above: In April 1934 the two IWCR Lancaster bogies were refurbished and formed into Set 501 for use on the Bembridge branch; alterations included the downgrading of some first class compartments to third. It was posed at Ryde St Johns, complete with Terrier locomotive No.9 *Fishbourne* and bearing the branch destination board. Also noteworthy are the 'Wood & Co' hoardings and the open space yet to be covered in houses. (Photo: A.B.MacLeod collection)

The Southern was clearly impressed with its Island investment and in June 1931 published the following information:

RAIL PROGRESS IN THE ISLE OF WIGHT SINCE THE ISLAND RAILWAYS WERE ABSORBED INTO THE SOUTHERN RAILWAY GROUP IN 1923

	1923	1931
Total Number of Engines	18	26
Total number of Carriages	107	160
Total Seating Capacity	3,722	5,628
Total number of trains on weekdays in Summer	170	256
Total number of trains on weekdays in Winter	140	186

These figures show that the present Winter Service in the Island is larger than the Summer Service used to be prior to the formation of the Southern Railway.

TRAFFIC TO AND FROM THE MAINLAND

	1927	1930
Total Number of Passengers	1,990,602	2,479,145
Total Number of Motor-cars	8,420	15,900

Above: The Freshwater branch was the preserve of A1X class Terrier locomotives until the permanent way was relaid and bridges strengthened, assisted latterly by two IWR 2-4-0T. Southern Railway import W3 *Carisbrooke* awaits departure Yarmouth with the 11.22am from Newport on 7th July 1930, hauling a Stroudley 4-set plus a loose third.   (Photo: A.B.MacLeod collection/A.W.Croughton)

Above: W30 taking water at Ventnor in July 1930, which also shows the simple coaling facilities of bagged coal on a raised platform and a wagonload of coal alongside. The photographer recorded that this was the 9.55am 'Sunday Only' working from Cowes, which accounts for the locomotive still carrying the Newport-Sandown headcode. Some other points of note are the new K1 Mark 235-type telephone box, the wall of the original turntable pit and the locomotive carrying both 3-link and screw couplings on the front hook. (Photo: P.C.Allen)

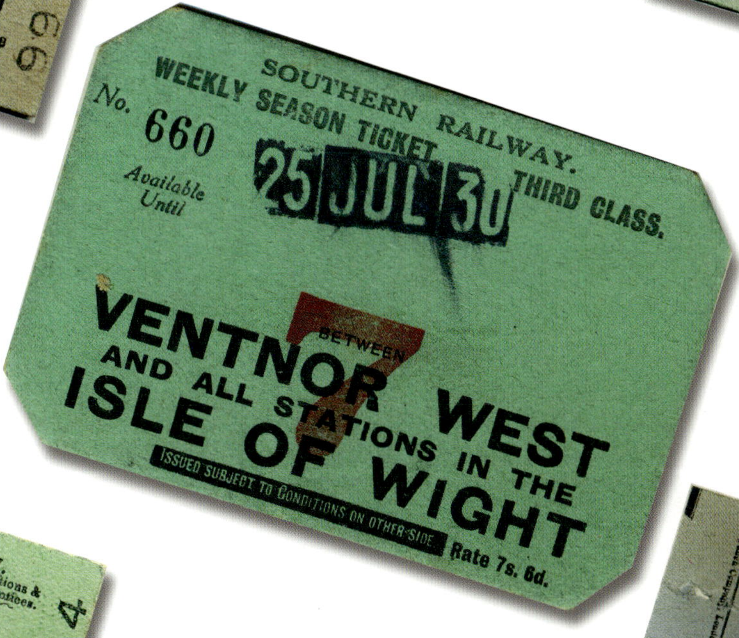

Above: E1 W3 *Ryde* stands in Ryde up yard at the head of Set 490, comprising three LSWR and three LCDR carriages, and an LSWR van. Mr Sweetman seems to be in contemplative mood, possibly regarding the star embellishment around the dart on W3.   (Photo: A.B.MacLeod)

Left: Photographs of goods trains, especially on the Freshwater branch, are rare. Terrier W10 *Cowes* heads a single wagon of coal and an LSWR brake van as it hurries through Calbourne station in the winter of 1931/2.   (Photo: A.B.MacLeod)

Chapter Eight
The Southern Comes To Vectis

In the 1920s the Isle of Wight had a plethora of independent bus companies which between them covered most of the Island. Vehicles and service frequency were of varying quality and the chance to provide a modern and reliable service was taken by one Frank Dodson who, in association with partners, founded *Dodson Bros. Ltd.*, trading as the *Vectis Bus Service*.

Vectis was aggressive in its tactics but inventive in matters of marketing, boasting, *'large, roomy vehicles, comfortably upholstered.....drivers are experienced men.....and the whole enterprise is excellently managed.'* Vectis did not have it all its own way: the local authorities who issued the licences were seriously concerned at excessive speed, damage to roads and aggressive tactics to secure customers.

Nationally, the availability of cheap road vehicles which could be converted to bus or truck use was precipitated by the end of the First World War in 1918, after which thousands of such units were available at knock-down prices. This proliferation nationally of road transport hit the railways hard: passenger numbers fell from 1579 million in 1920 to 1232 million in 1925; freight loads dropped from 318 million to 304 million over the same period. There was little by way of regulation to stem the flow.

The Southern Railway's reaction could be regarded as *'if you can't beat 'em, join 'em!'* and they sought powers to operate their own buses. This came by way of the Southern Railway (Road Transport) Act of 1928. The Southern's first action was to acquire financial interest in associated bus operators. One of their first agreements was with National Omnibus & Transport Co. in the West-country from which was created the *Southern National Co.* in 1928.

Back on the Island, in March 1929, Dodson Brothers shares were purchased by the Southern, giving them a major interest in the *Vectis Bus Service* and Gilbert Szlumper, former Docks & Marine Manager and now Assistant SR General Manager and Charles de Pury, Assistant to Divisional Officers (IW) became Board members. On the 27th August 1929 the *Southern Vectis Omnibus Co. Ltd.* (SVCo) was registered as a private company with its

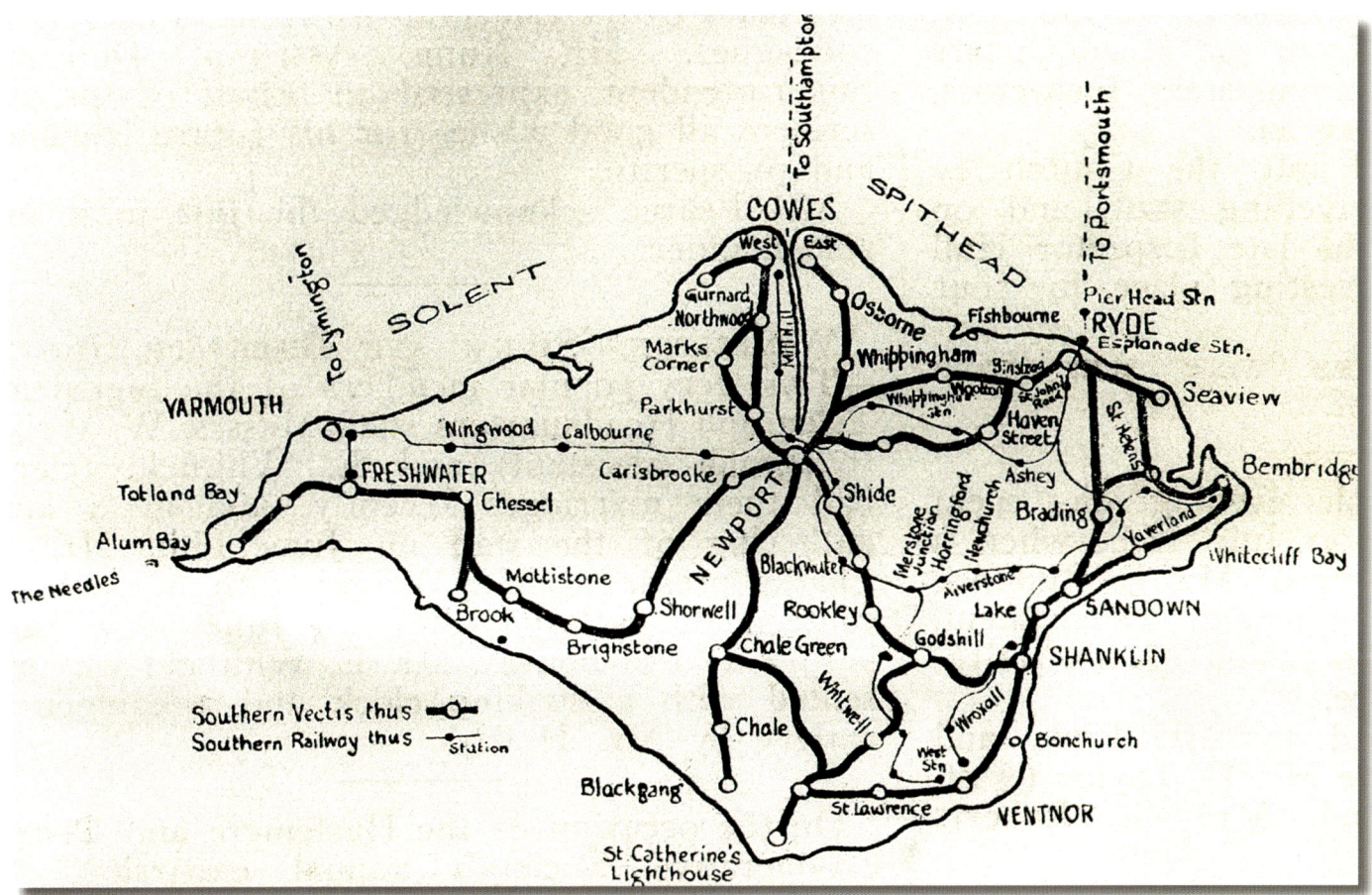

Above: A map of the Isle of Wight, showing principal bus routes operated by the newly created *Southern Vectis*. Railway routes are in lighter lines.

(A.B.MacLeod collection)

(A.B.MacLeod collection)

headquarters at Waterloo station. This was formed to carry on the Vectis business. Three Dodson brothers were amongst the Board members, which also included Charles de Pury, who was succeeded by Alistair MacLeod when he became responsible for all matters regarding the Island's railways in 1930.

In 1989, Richard Newman wrote an excellent book, *Southern Vectis-The First 60 Years* and A.B. MacLeod provided the Foreword in which he outlined his position within the bus industry thus, *"In 1930, I was called to Waterloo and told by Sir Herbert (Walker) that I was to be given further responsibilities by the addition of the Traffic and Commercial departments, and would be given the title of 'Assistant for the Isle of Wight' with headquarters in Newport. This post included a directorship of THE SOUTHERN VECTIS OMNIBUS COMPANY LTD., which had been newly purchased by the Southern Railway from the Dodson brothers, and was placed under the Chairmanship of the SR Assistant General Manager, G.S. Szlumper.*

In fact for a short time the SR had complete financial control of the Vectis Company which had started privately in 1921. I can remember going with the other directors to choose the new colour and lettering for the Company's vehicles; on another occasion to inspect the new garage accommodating 100 buses. This might seem rather ostentatious but by 1933 the company had a fleet of 66 vehicles, most of the latest design.

The SR issued a 7s 6d All Island Weekly Season ticket which covered the 32 stations and, at 15s 6d, the steamers from Ryde to Southsea and Portsmouth; the accompanying folder included a map of the Island showing railways and SVOC bus routes and places of interest to be visited. There was also a SR 'Hints for Holidays' yearly guide with a full page SVOC advertisement giving the advantages of travel by bus on their 14 routes; one of these stated 'The buses provide comfort and adequate protection in all weathers'. I always wondered if this was a subtle way of suggesting that the railway carriages were subject to leaking roofs and windows!

My personal involvement in Isle of Wight transport sadly ended in the summer of 1934 when I was promoted to Waterloo."

The 1930 Road Transport Act's regulatory nature made life a whole lot harder for the smaller bus companies, and on the Island in the 10 years from 1929 no fewer than 14 independents sold out to *Southern Vectis*. To get the full picture of Island bus history during the Southern Vectis period the aforementioned volume by Richard Newman, and his subsequent *Southern Vectis 1929 - 2004* should provide all you need.

The Dodson brothers sold their interests in the SVCo to the *Tilling & British Automobile Traction Group* in 1932 and in October that year a working group of joint SVOC and SR members, including Alistair MacLeod, formed a Standing Joint Committee (SJC) to oversee liaison and business development between the two companies. From the Minute Books of the SJC it appears that principal activity was regarding distribution of publicity, timetables and matters relating to interavailability of tickets. This latter subject reached epic proportions in terms of published conditions and complication, particularly with regard to routeing and acceptability of outward and return halves of tickets. How the average customer, let alone the staff, understood what they could use where and when is a total mystery!

In addition to the mundane there were the occasional highlights: one potentially sticky problem was dealt with at the SJC as follows, 'Agreed that the SVCo should convey Messers Lyons & Co's Pastry Traffic to consignees in villages in outlying districts served by the company's omnibus. The traffic to be handed over by the Railway Company, a flat rate of 4d per package being allowed the Vectis Company.' This entry was followed by a list of near station collection points one of which was 'Traffic for St Helens - To be picked up by 'buses passing St Helens

station"…. a mischievous mind might imagine cartons of cream cones being grabbed by a loop handle at speed by a passing conductor!

Mac took up the cause for Seaview with regard to ticket agency and after some months managed to arrange for *Watsons Estate Agents* to act for both the Railway and Bus companies. Not surprising really as MacLeod lived nearby and as a pillar of the local community and respected member of the Seaview Sailing Club probably had little choice other than to champion the matter if he wanted to stay afloat.

Various agreements were reached with regard to the use of station yards and premises by SVOC buses. Of particular note was the use of the Bembridge Toll road, owned by the Southern; surprisingly the Railway agreed a charge of £100 for bus usage for twelve months up to 28th February 1933, a sum which did not change for over 20 years!

Some light at the end of one particular tunnel came at the meeting of 20th September 1933 when the following appeared:
'Advertising - A draft handbill containing reference to all the interavailability arrangements that have been agreed to date was produced and it was AGREED that a supply of these be ordered, the cost of printing to be shared equally by the two Companies. Messrs Budd and MacLeod undertook to arrange distribution'…. At last!

A final extract from the meeting of 15th May 1934, Minute S.V.79 under the heading Membership of Committee contained, inter alia, the following: 'The Secretary reported he had received a letter from the Secretary of the Southern Railway Company, dated 26th April, 1934, in which it was stated that the present Southern Railway Representatives, Mr H.A.Short and Mr A.B.MacLeod, had resigned their positions as from 30th April 1934.' MacLeod was on his way back to the mainland with a promotion.

For a man with an interest in matters transport, and a predilection for photography, it is surprising that, in a letter to Richard Newman, MacLeod admitted he had only ever taken two pictures of buses, both of which were reproduced in Richard's 1989 book. Quite what this says about the man, we don't know.....maybe the leaking roof and windows comment earlier had a greater effect on MacLeod than first thought.

SOUTHERN VECTIS
OMNIBUS COMPANY LIMITED
In association with the Southern Railway.

LIST OF MOTOR BUS SERVICES.

Service No.   Route.
- *1. Newport and Ventnor.
- *2. Newport and West Cowes.
- *3. Ryde, Shanklin and Godshill.
- 4. Newport and Carisbrooke.
- *5. Newport and Ryde.
- 6. Newport and East Cowes.
- *7. Shanklin, Bonchurch and Ventnor.
- *8. Newport, Freshwater, Totland and Alum Bay via Shorwell and Brighstone.
- 9. Cowes and Gurnard.
- *10. Newport, Shanklin and Sandown.
- 11. Ventnor to Whiteley Bank via Wroxall.
- 12. Ventnor, St. Catherine's Lighthouse and Blackgang.
- 13. Chale and Newport.
- 14. Ryde, Seaview and St. Helens.
- 15. East Cowes and Ryde.

Local Office: SOUTHERN VECTIS OMNIBUS CO., LTD.
19, St. James' Square, Newport, I.W.
Telephone: NEWPORT 216.

The main points of advantage of travelling by Southern Vectis 'buses in order to view the beauty spots of the Island may be summed up as follows :—

(1) Passengers have the choice of times by which they may travel on any 'bus, joining and alighting at any point along the particular route they desire, whilst the linking up of services at Newport and Godshill provides a ready means of interchange of trips—distinct advantages over the accepted type of motor excursion which has a set time of departure and keeps to a prescribed route.

(2) The linking up of services at Newport and Godshill renders the whole of the Island easily accessible. Remote districts are served, and the little known Southern coast of the Island may be readily explored.

(3) The 'buses provide comfort and adequate protection in all weathers.

(4) Passengers who have travelled on the Outward journey by 'Bus on routes marked * may, if they wish, make the return journey by RAIL from principal stations at no extra charge. For details see Time Table.

In corresponding with Advertisers, please mention "Hints for Holidays."
105

Left: The Southern Vectis advert from *Hints for Holidays* with which MacLeod was less than impressed.
(A.B.MacLeod collection)

Chapter Nine
To Waterloo

The year 1934 was not the best for Alistair MacLeod; his cherished locomotive *Ryde* was destined for the scrap-heap despite his, and others, best efforts to save it. On the career front, he was relocated back to the mainland to take up the post of Assistant Western Divisional Loco Running Superintendent; this unexpected move came as a knock-on to the death of the Divisional Superintendent who had fallen from a train! One small benefit was the Lynton & Barnstaple, the Southern's own main line in miniature, a narrow gauge line which was sadly in its last years as Mac came on the scene but, he did find time to photograph engines and rolling stock and to enjoy the delights of the Devon countryside from the cabs of most of the locomotives. However, this and further promotion to Assistant to the Locomotive Running Superintendent was only partial compensation for losing what MacLeod described as *"The best job in the world"*. In 1990, Ian Allan wrote of Mac's Island tenure, *"There he was king of his own castle, with a magnificent real train set all of his very own."*

During 1938 Alistair accepted the position of Assistant Stores Superintendent and this move was to set the course for the rest of his career in the railway industry. Driving desks was not Mac's favourite occupation and his new position may have lacked the attractions of the Locomotive Department but, as Alan Blackburn put it, *"Remember also that the Grouping had produced a 'surplus' of senior staff and the loco running side was no exception. Walker needed a good man for this job and Mac was that man"*. He was further promoted to Southern Railway's Stores Superintendent in 1945. Whilst on the face of it one would be forgiven for thinking this was a glorified storekeeper's job, it did in fact represent a position of considerable responsibility and influence in which MacLeod was well respected.

In 1945 Alistair moved his family to a new home in Wimbledon and a comprehensive '0' gauge railway occupied two rooms on the top floor. Winter Sundays saw the 'boys' operating pre-1923 timetables on the layout and, as Ewan writes, *"The construction of clockwork locomotives and rolling stock continued unabated after A's return home from Waterloo in the evenings."*

"As the family grew up and demanded more space," Ewan recalls, *"it was necessary to return one room to domestic use and the England portion of the layout was dismantled. The multi-layered Scottish system continued for many years more, but became increasingly rivalled in leisure time by the 7¼inch Greywood Central Railway (GCR) in John Samuel's garden at Walton - on - Thames.*

Above: A.B.MacLeod and team in full decontamination gear, in an official photograph, probably in the sidings at Waterloo in 1939.
(Photo: E.MacLeod collection)

Right: Every book needs a mystery picture...and this is ours! It's dated 1944; Mac is on the right but quite who the Stan Laurel look-alike is, or the other gentleman, we have no idea, nor do we know where they were or what they were doing!
(Photo: E.MacLeod collection)

Above: The back garden of the new house in Parkside Gardens, Wimbledon, taken by Alistair in 1945.   (Photo: E.MacLeod collection)

The sitting room table on winter evenings was now more likely to serve as a bench for painting a wagon or GCR lineside notice than '0' gauge!."

Winter weekends were now largely infrastructure dominated; designing, building, digging, clearing and concreting, with summer weekends employed in all the tasks of operating a 7¼inch gauge steam railway. Appropriate Health & Safety regulations were drawn up, both to safeguard the band of enthusiasts, but also the trickle of visitors who queued outside Samuel's back gate to get a glimpse and, hopefully, a ride and which increased significantly as word got round. Nationalisation of the railways was a further chance for Mac, from his official position, to secure artefacts from the past and he wasted no time in January 1948 writing to W.H.Austen of the newly-acquired Kent & East Sussex Railway asking after items of historic interest.

Mac was also beavering away behind the scenes with the Waterloo Centenary event, and with a small team he selected LSWR T3 Class loco No.563 from the scrap line at Kimbridge for display. They made the selection on site on the 4th May and by 28th of the month the loco was at Eastleigh with a tube change and base coat painting well under way. The event was to be opened by Herbert Walker on 14th June, so there was little time for delay,

and whilst Helen McKie had many months to prepare her wonderful *Waterloo Centenary* posters and cover for the illustrated booklet, the painters at Eastleigh must have been really at their wits end with the tri-composite coach and locomotive. A little tacky varnish could be forgiven! After the event the T3 led a somewhat peripatetic existence whilst its fate was decided and it finally joined the National Collection.

However, Nationalisation was to bring greater career choices but Mac was clearly type-cast, becoming Stores Superintendent for British Railways London Midland Region, based at Euston, where he described his position as the *'Biggest buyer of materials in Britain'*. In addition to the prestige, there was for Mac another less obvious side to being a Senior Officer; Ewan MacLeod recalls that his father was particularly amused at staff reaction when using his medallion travel pass; Alistair related tales of staff failure to recognise it and their various reactions when enlightened as to its all-encompassing authority to travel and his position within the Railway hierarchy.

This was to be the end of the line career-wise, but with a new title of Supplies & Contracts Manager, in 1965 Mac retired with 44 years' service. Next - stop? Shepperton, and a job with old friend Ian Allan.

Left: An extract from *Rail News* June 1965. (Courtesy *Rail News*. E.MacLeod collection)

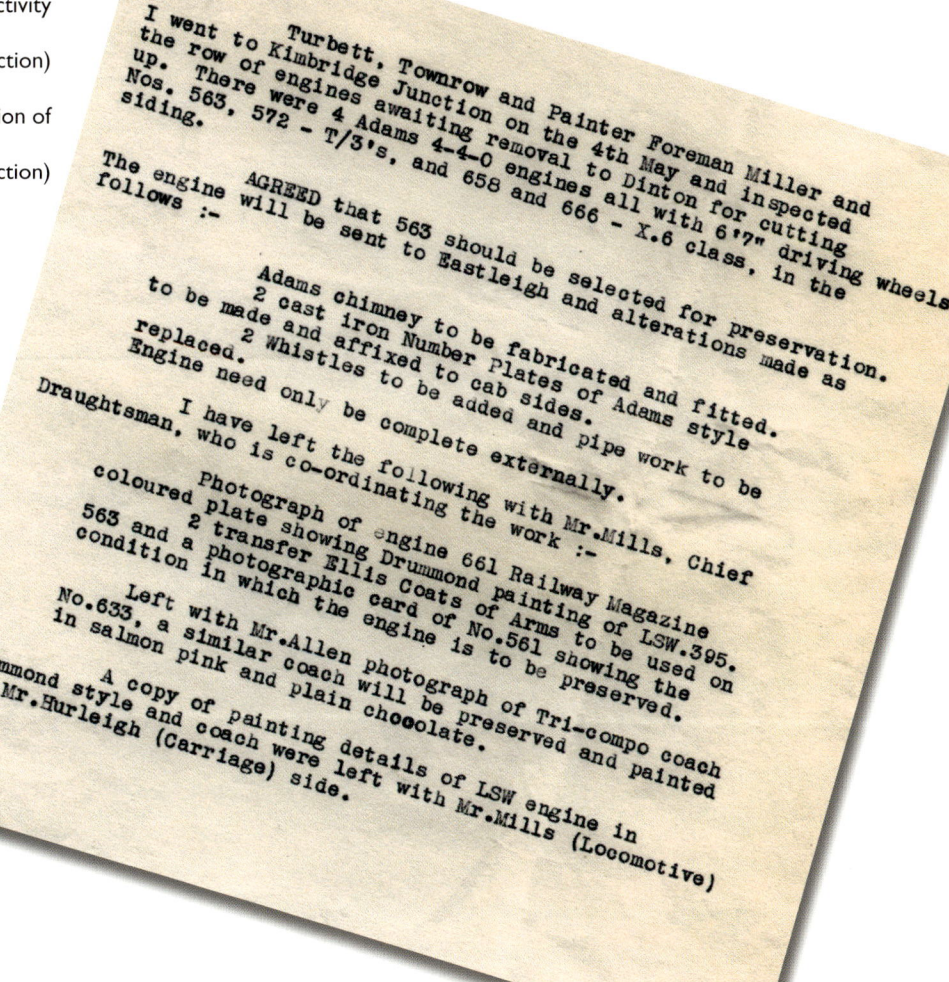

Above: On 28th May 1948 there is fevered activity on ex-LSWR Class T3, at Eastleigh.
(Photo: E.MacLeod collection)

Right: MacLeod's own notes as to the selection of 563 at Kimbridge and subsequent work.
(Photo: E.MacLeod collection)

Turbett, Townrow and Painter Foreman Miller and I went to Kimbridge Junction on the 4th May and inspected the row of engines awaiting removal to Dinton for cutting up. There were 4 Adams 4-4-0 engines all with 6'7" driving wheels. Nos. 563, 572 - T/3's, and 658 and 666 - X.6 class, in the siding.

AGREED that 563 should be selected for preservation. The engine will be sent to Eastleigh and alterations made as follows :-

Adams chimney to be fabricated and fitted.
2 cast iron Number Plates of Adams style to be made and affixed to cab sides.
2 Whistles to be added and pipe work to be replaced.
Engine need only be complete externally.

I have left the following with Mr.Mills, Chief Draughtsman, who is co-ordinating the work :-

Photograph of engine 661 Railway Magazine coloured plate showing Drummond painting of LSW.395.
2 transfer Ellis Coats of Arms to be used on 563 and a photographic card of No.561 showing the condition in which the engine is to be preserved.

Left with Mr.Allen photograph of Tri-compo coach No.633, a similar coach will be preserved and painted in salmon pink and plain chocolate.

A copy of painting details of LSW engine in Drummond style and coach were left with Mr.Mills (Locomotive) and Mr.Hurleigh (Carriage) side.

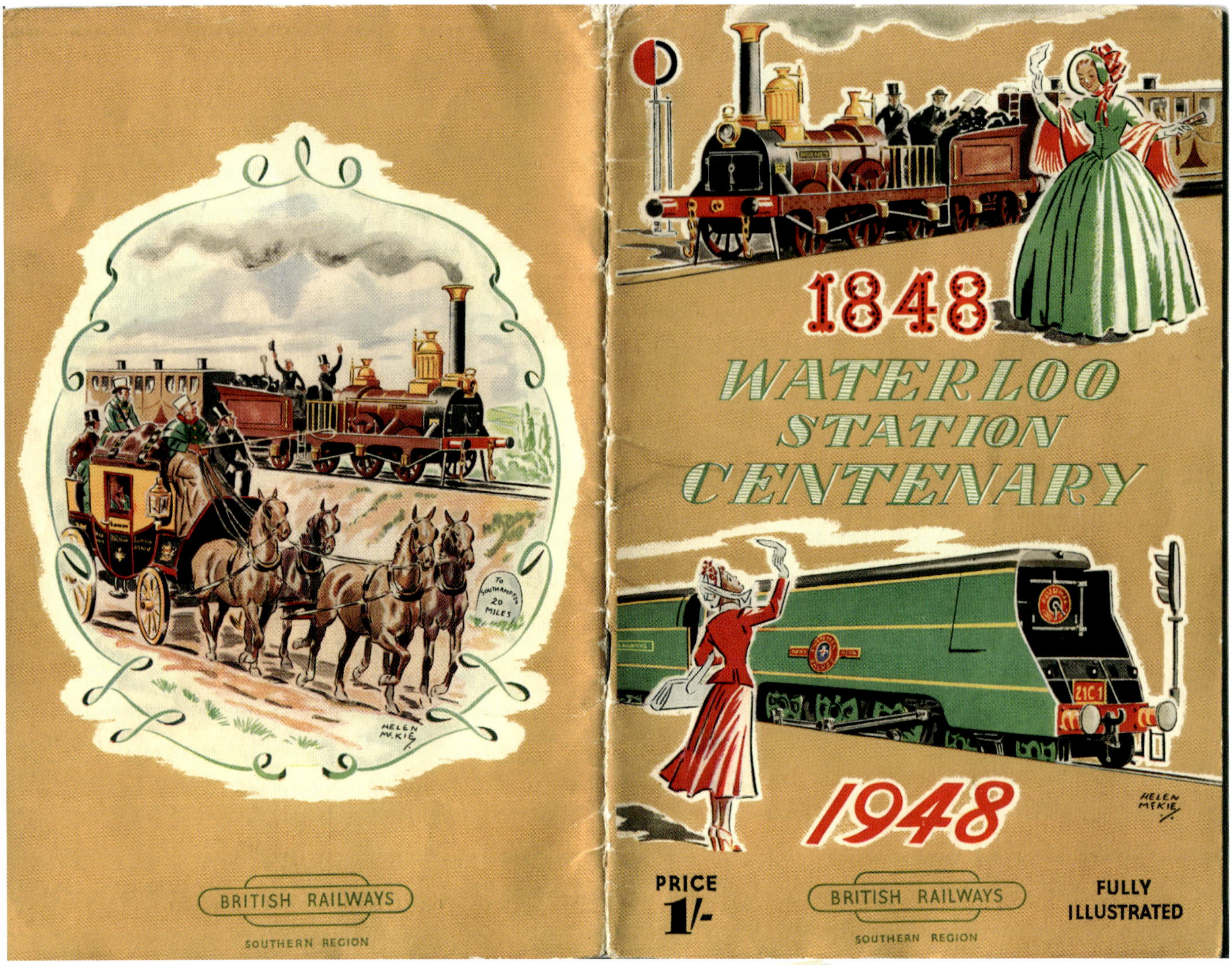

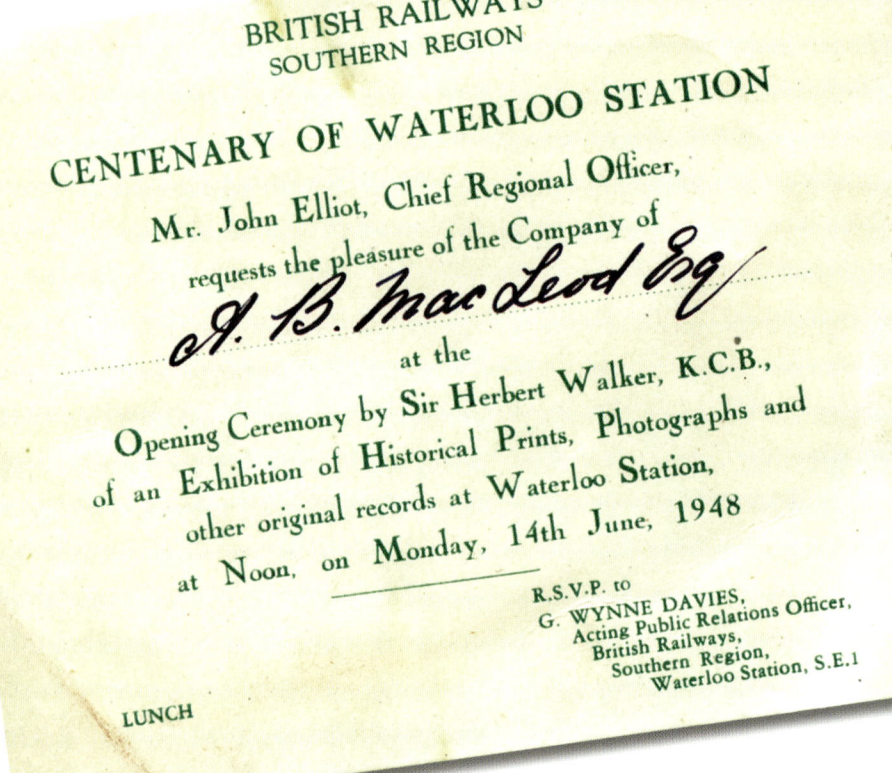

Top: The cover of the Waterloo Centenary booklet with wonderful artwork by Helen McKie.
(Courtesy National Railway Museum/SSPL)

BRITISH RAILWAYS
SOUTHERN REGION

CENTENARY OF WATERLOO STATION

Mr. John Elliot, Chief Regional Officer,
requests the pleasure of the Company of
A. B. MacLeod Esq
at the
Opening Ceremony by Sir Herbert Walker, K.C.B.,
of an Exhibition of Historical Prints, Photographs and
other original records at Waterloo Station,
at Noon, on Monday, 14th June, 1948

R.S.V.P. to
G. WYNNE DAVIES,
Acting Public Relations Officer,
British Railways,
Southern Region,
Waterloo Station, S.E.1

LUNCH

Left: A happy occasion was Mac's invitation to the Waterloo centenary celebrations, in marked contrast to the sombre gathering at Paddington four years later (opposite).
(E.MacLeod collection)

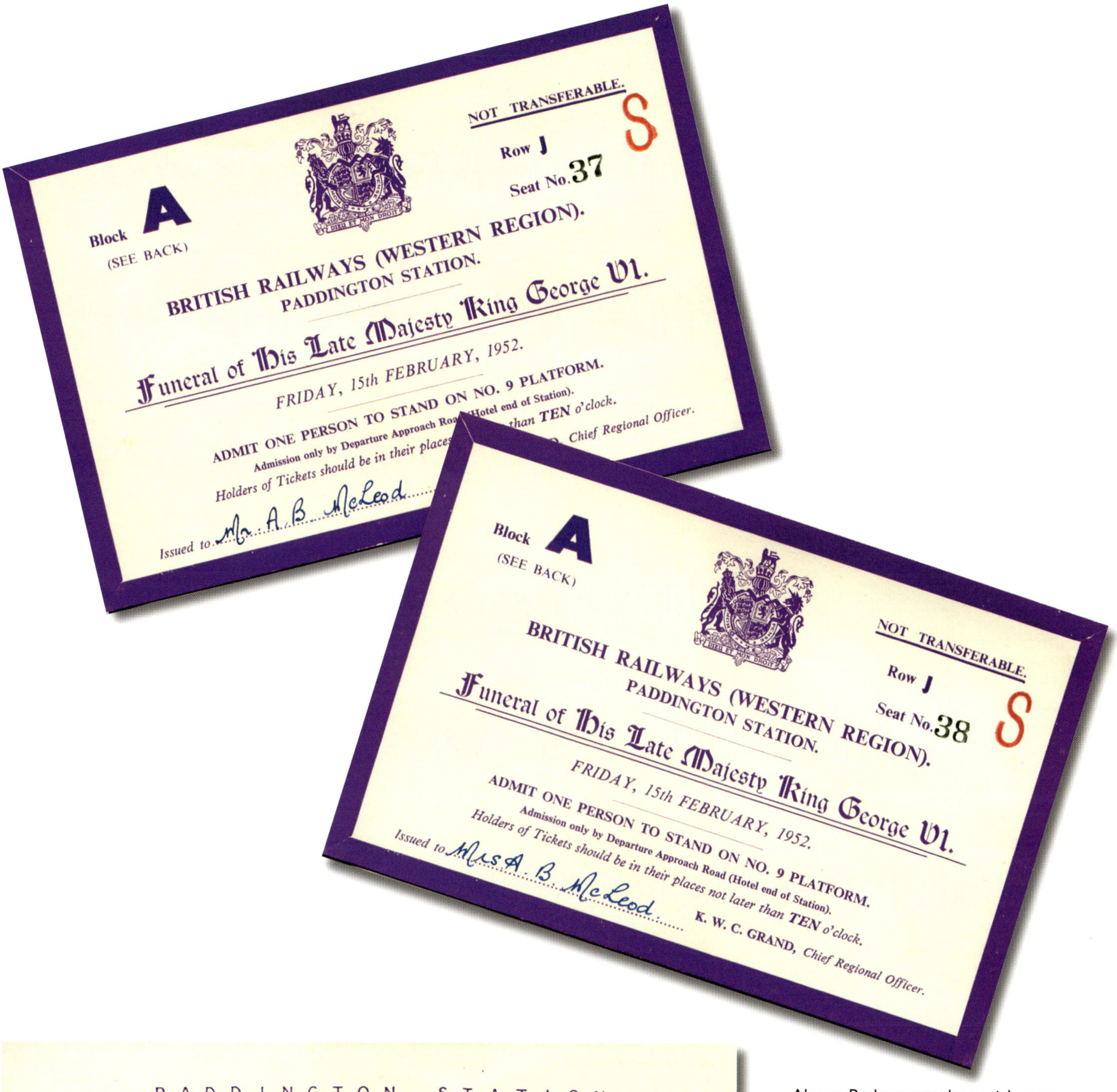

NOT TRANSFERABLE.

Row J

Seat No. **37**

S

Block **A**

(SEE BACK)

BRITISH RAILWAYS (WESTERN REGION).
PADDINGTON STATION.

Funeral of His Late Majesty King George VI.

FRIDAY, 15th FEBRUARY, 1952.

ADMIT ONE PERSON TO STAND ON NO. 9 PLATFORM.

Admission only by Departure Approach Road (Hotel end of Station).

Holders of Tickets should be in their places ~~than~~ TEN o'clock.

K. W. C. GRAND, Chief Regional Officer.

Issued to *Mr. A. B. McLeod*

Block **A**

(SEE BACK)

BRITISH RAILWAYS (WESTERN REGION).
PADDINGTON STATION.

NOT TRANSFERABLE.

Row J

Seat No. **38**

S

Funeral of His Late Majesty King George VI.

FRIDAY, 15th FEBRUARY, 1952.

ADMIT ONE PERSON TO STAND ON NO. 9 PLATFORM.

Admission only by Departure Approach Road (Hotel end of Station).

Holders of Tickets should be in their places not later than TEN o'clock.

Issued to *Mrs A. B. McLeod*

K. W. C. GRAND, Chief Regional Officer.

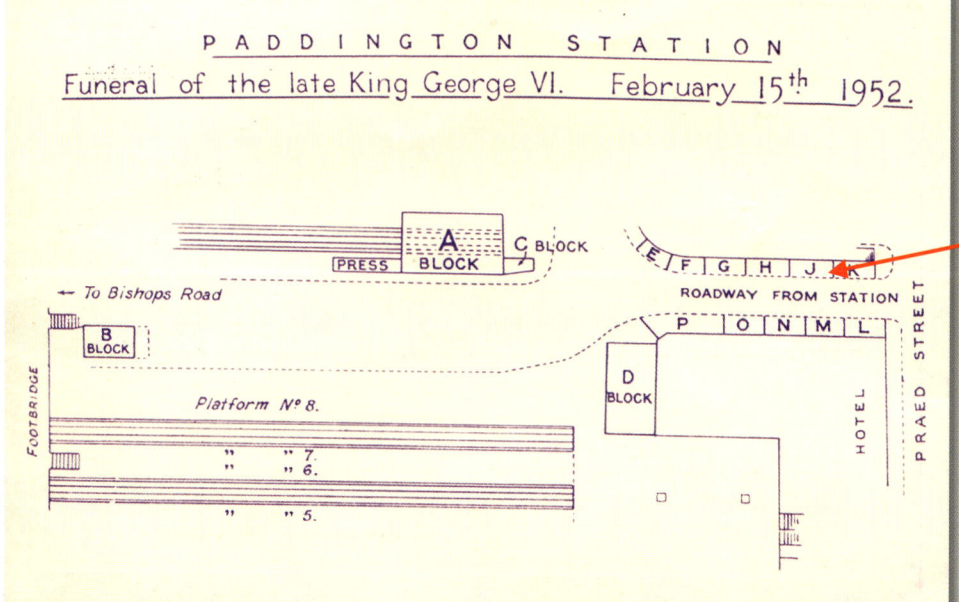

Above: Perhaps not the social event of 1952, Mr & Mrs MacLeod's invitation to that part of the funeral arrangements for the late King George VI which took place at Paddington station. Their seating area is arrowed on the left.

(Photo: E.MacLeod collection)

Chapter Ten
Shepperton and Chertsey

Ian Allan was born at Christ's Hospital School and as he put it, *"went through the usual run of middle class education, kindergarten, prep school and eventually to St Paul's"*. Whilst there at the tender age of 15, an injury to his right knee cost him his leg but undaunted he returned to school before searching for employment.

Early in 1939 he was offered a post as a Grade 5 Clerk with the Southern Railway at Waterloo and started work in the Publicity & Public Relations Department on 16th July

1939. Ian took full advantage of his position and, with the unofficial help of the office pass, indulged his fascination with railways to the full, including walking the length of the Waterloo & City Railway in traffic ..tin leg and all!

It dawned on him that there was a growing interest in the operations of the Southern and of locomotives and stock in particular. He suggested to his line manager the production of a booklet containing such information and a list of locomotive numbers. This was promptly rebuffed but as Ian stated, *"I sought an audience of the Public Relations Officer himself, one Cuthbert Grasemann."* It was agreed Ian could publish on his own account and was warned it was at his own risk and expense. Immediately after distribution started Grasemann summoned Allan to his office and ordered him to withdraw the book. It appeared that none other than O.V.S.Bulleid had objected to the publication of details of 'his' domain and Grasemann clearly caved under the weight of a Bulleid. Threatened with the sack if he failed to comply, Allan, with a distinct sense of 'all or nothing', sent a copy to the Company Chairman who responded with a highly commendatory letter congratulating the author ..deflation of stout parties! The future of the publication was assured although co-operation from the C.M.E.'s offices was no longer forthcoming.

Thus the Ian Allan story began and our main man, Alistair Balmain MacLeod, is about to enter the frame. Ian decided to extend his operations and tackle a similar publication on the Great Western Railway, as he put it, *"with disastrous results."*... as with anything Great Western this is better left to others to tell another day.

Ian Allan takes up the story, *"I was sent for by 'Mr MacLeod' to go to Waterloo's Room 20. A.B.MacLeod was a senior officer and Southern Railway Magazine contributor and, I was to discover, a dedicated nut when it came to railways. "Do the LMS" he ordered in his whimsically humorous way but I was hesitant as I knew nothing about the*

Left: Ewan MacLeod's personal copy of a 1947 edition *ABC of LMS Locomotives*, written largely by his father. (Courtesy Ian Allan Publishing)

LMS;..........*Mindful of the trouble with Mr Bulleid, I was cautious but Mac said he would prepare the text if I could get the blessing and the pictures.*

Parents came in useful; they were on friendly terms with the local butcher, George Reeves, in Staines; aforesaid butcher was the royal warrant holder to supply meat to Windsor Castle. Lord Wigram was the grand panjandrum who oversaw the meat in the royal apartments or something but, more importantly, he was a director of the LMS. So bingo, out came all the pictures, dimensions and details of the LMS fleet. All were fed up to Room 20 and the first LMS book appeared. Generously the real author agreed to our joint names appearing on the cover though he had really done all the work for which he expected no recompense, other than the brief acknowledgement of his contribution."

MacLeod, popularly known within the Ian Allan fraternity as *Uncle Mac*, was clearly pleased with his first venture into 'puffer-nutter' publication and wanted to further disseminate his knowledge with a second book, *The McIntosh Locomotives of the Caledonian Railway*. Allan was unsure of this venture but felt some form of obligation to publish and later wrote, *"Uncle Mac had been rewarded: this highly expensive production at 3s 6d was really my thank you to him as it actually lost money and I began to realise that in publishing you don't win 'em all."*

The authors feel that in fairness to Uncle Mac it needs to be added that Mr Allan saw fit to re-print the Caledonian locomotives book in 1948, albeit with additional photographs and a change of date to Mac's original introduction. Readers may therefore draw their own conclusions as to its viability.

Perhaps mistakenly Alistair may have felt he had found another outlet for his latent authoristic talent besides his regular magazine contributions and summoned Ian to Room 20 again, this time suggesting *"You must now start doing some proper casebound books"*. Horrified, and in the knowledge of what MacLeod's own book had cost, he put up more than a little resistance but Uncle Mac persisted and they settled on a book about named

expresses on Britain's railways. Who to write it? Mac insisted Cecil J. Allen (no relation to any of the other numerous Allans, Allens etc. who appear in this book). Allan, that's Ian, was aghast that he, a lowly clerk should approach a great doyen of railway literature, but with Mac's prod did so and further embarrassed himself by holding their meetings in Allan's office with colleagues listening in.

David Allan, Ian's son, advised that Alistair had authored

Above: Alistair MacLeod's first solo publication.   (Courtesy Ian Allan Publishing)

Below: Alistair MacLeod originally made and later rescued this small notice from the Greywood Central Railway, retaining it as a keepsake and reminder of earlier endeavours.
(E.MacLeod collection)

a number of works for Ian Allan but clearly a conflict of interest was appearing using railway material for a private company and his authoring ceased .. at least officially and his name no longer appeared on books. As the War ended in 1945 Ian Allan felt it was time to go it alone and Ian Allan Ltd was incorporated on 1st November 1945.

After Uncle Mac's retirement in 1965 he became a frequent visitor to Ian Allan's offices at Shepperton where he found the Ian Allan library in some disarray and promptly set about the vast collection of material, bringing order to his world. After a while he became a daily visitor and received his free lunch in their Pullman car *MALAGA* which he felt was a fair exchange for his services. Ian Allan, writing in 1992, recalls an unfortunate side effect of this action, *"There were very high fallutin' and technical conversations between him, (Mac.) Charles Klapper and Basil Cooper, a well known railway writer ..... they soon had everyone else buying sandwiches in the pub rather than face an hour or even half an hour as a passive audience listening to the merits and demerits of the enlarged bunkers on the O2 Class locomotives or the number of rivets in a King's tender."*

UNDER SECTION 3 OF THE TRAFFIC ACT ALL PASSENGERS ARE EXPECTED TO PAY FOR THEIR TICKETS. OTHERWISE MR MACLEOD WILL BE ON THEIR TRACK. BY ORDER.

GREYWOOD CENTRAL RAILWAY

"THE WEEK-END LINE."

President:
J. O. C. SAMUEL

Vice Presidents :
A. B. MacLEOD
WALT DISNEY

Secretary & Catering Manager:
C. M. HOYT

Head Office :
GREYWOOD NORTH
BURWOOD PARK
WALTON ON THAMES
ENGLAND

Telephone:
Walton-on-Thames 1724.

Telegrams :
Steamwell Greywood, Walton.

Chief Mechanical Engineer:
M. PHILLIP SIMPSON

Chief Civil Engineer:
DENIS V BAGLOW

Locomotive Superintendent:
C. J. BISHOP

Public Relations Officer:
HAROLD P. JEFFERY

Uncle Mac ruled the Library with a rod of iron, David Allan remembered; he set up a desk in a central location but always managed to appear from a dark corner behind any person who had failed to check in with him. At one point he forbad access to any but Editors and this edict was enforced for quite some time.

Mac and Ian Allan were both keen on miniature railways; MacLeod had previously introduced

Left: Another page from one of Alistair MacLeod's albums, this time including the top of a sheet of Greywood Central notepaper upon which both Mac and Walt Disney share equal billing! The photograph depicts a busy, but obviously staged view of the Greywood sheds. A.B.MacLeod is the person attending the locomotive on the turntable.

(E.MacLeod collection)

himself to Jack Howey of the RHDR whilst visiting his wife's family who lived nearby, and became a regular helper.

Ian Allan had taken on the role of publicity agent for the RHDR and was also actively involved. One day Mac invited Ian to Walton and the home of the late Sir John Samuel where they viewed the Greywood Central Railway meandering through about an acre of the estate. Mac had been heavily involved with the line for some time prior to this and knew his way around; he was in fact a Vice President, an honour he shared with none other than Walt Disney and whose gift to Mac of a signed animation cell of Donald Duck remains with the MacLeod family to this day. The point of the visit soon became clear, Ian wrote, *"Pinkie Samuel, John's widow, had decided to sell the house and did not know what to do with the railway. "Could you," asked Mac, "find a home for it?" I demurred."*

Allan and a couple of partners had by now become operators of the Hastings Miniature Railway and were also the rather speculative owners of a 56 acre plot near Chertsey... possibly a home for the Greywood Central line? Ian recalled, *"Mac came to view it, deemed it suitable and to the land owners' united amazement a week later they found a complete railway literally dumped on their land."* Mac made his way to Ian's office, complete with Southern Railway notebook which contained a complete inventory of the Greywood kit. The conversation was vague to say the least and Ian later wrote, *"It took me a little while to rumble what he was on about."* until at last Mac said, *"So if you will let me have your cheque, I will give it to Lady Samuel."* As far as Ian was concerned he was just finding a home, the idea of purchase was never an issue!

In the end a deal was done and a new company, Ian Allan (Miniature Railway Supplies) Ltd, was conceived with the broader ambition of providing equipment for commercial use. Mac designed a simple 0-4-0 diesel locomotive for the company and later a much bigger locomotive which found favour at their lines in Whitby, Bournemouth, Sandown I.W., Prestatyn, Buxton and Bognor. The line at Hastings also came into the fold.

In Chertsey the Greywood line took shape, the nearby Cockcrow Hill lending its name to the new line, conveniently retaining the GCR initials in the Great Cockcrow Railway and honouring the original owner John Samuel's interest in the Great Central Railway. Uncle Mac was to remain a regular visitor and driver, particularly of

Above: 'Uncle Mac' in his later years at the controls of his diesel locomotive *Winifred* with a well loaded train on the Great Cockcrow Railway.
(Photo: E.MacLeod collection)

Overleaf: Pride of place in MacLeod's album, a page of colour pictures of the Great Cockcrow Railway locomotive named in his honour.
(E.MacLeod collection)

Right: Part of the Brighton Toy Museum collection is MacLeod's Caledonian Railway No.54. This is a scratchbuilt model of a McIntosh Class 55 locomotive. The prototype was designed specifically to haul heavy passenger trains between Stirling, Callander and Oban. Built by the Caledonian at St Rollox in 1905, there were only nine engines in this class.　　　(Photo: R.Silsbury)

his 0-6-0 diesel shunter, named *Winifred* after his wife. This locomotive had been specially built for him as he was, in later years, having difficulty in managing a steam engine. Later a Hymek type locomotive was named *A.B. MacLeod* in his honour. After Uncle Mac's death in 1990, his miniature locomotives remained at the Great Cockcrow Railway.

During his lifetime, Mac developed half a dozen or more '0' gauge layouts, all based on pre-grouping periods, and his son Ewan advises there were well over 100 clockwork locomotives and many carriages and wagons. Many were conversions but many more were scratch built. These Mac disposed of during the 1970s and '80s; a few items were accepted for display at the National Railway Museum, others passing to family friends and like-minded collectors.

With the benefit of hindsight one thing becomes clear; Mac's rebuilds of the full size vehicles on the Isle of Wight were the product of a fertile and imaginative brain, resembling closely the way he approached model railways. MacLeod would have been no friend to Bing and Bassett-Lowke; since an early age he had taken proprietary models and converted them to resemble lesser known examples from north of the Border, tinplate six wheeler carriages, 'cut and shut' into bogies and various tender locomotive conversions are just some

Above: Also in the Brighton Toy Museum is Caledonian Railway No.816. Regarded as the McIntosh standard goods engine, the first 17 of the class were Westinghouse fitted and painted in passenger blue livery. This batch was employed on fast services between Glasgow Central, Gourock and Wemyss Bay. No.816 was built at St Rollox in 1899.
MacLeod's model is of particularly interesting construction; the frame is a shortened Bassett-Lowke item with original mechanism and running gear. Above the running plate is scratch built. The tender started life as a Bing product but has been modified at the frames and coal space. The dumb buffer wagon probably has Milbro origins but the brake van is less obvious and may be scratchbuilt. It was certainly painted by MacLeod in his very distinctive hand worked style.　　　(Photo: R.Silsbury)

Above: Another former MacLeod item in the Brighton Toy Museum is Caledonian Railway No.142. The distinctive Bing tender gives away the origins of this Bassett-Lowke retailed model of a MacIntosh 140 or Dunalastair IV Class. The twelve-inch-to-the-foot version was built for express passenger work in 1904 at St Rollox workshops and was one of 19 in the Class.   (Photo: R.Silsbury)

surviving examples. Ewan MacLeod comments:

"....my father was very keen to achieve correct scale, dimensional accuracy and livery. He acknowledged two types of railway modellers – the purists whose models were nigh on perfection, very detailed, and mainly for static exhibition; secondly those whose models were primarily part of a working railway. His interest was very much in the latter category."

Some of the models which Mac converted are, in their original form, collectors items and command very high prices. In consequence his efforts do not necessarily meet with the approval of all enthusiasts today, some of whom have been noted raising a disapproving eyebrow at them. The authors have managed to track down a selection to Christopher Littledale's Brighton Toy & Model Museum, including four locomotives and half a dozen carriages and wagons. Here they are safely housed for posterity and a selection of them is generally on display, although not identified as MacLeod's work. The Caledonian hand-painted livery is often a useful clue as to their origins.

A further interesting and somewhat larger survival is a 7¼inch gauge 2-8-0, S160 American austerity locomotive. Quite how it came into MacLeod's ownership is not clear but it was originally constructed by one Captain Saul in 1946. According to his daughter, Saul's interest in the class was aroused during the 1940s when transporting the full size items to this country from the U.S.A. Surprisingly, it appears that Uncle Mac did not run the locomotive at Greywood but sold it on to Mr L.H.Willoughby in Eastleigh, in 1965. It was Mr Willoughby who rebuilt the S160 and first named it *A.B.MacLeod*. After passing to a new owner in Lancing in 1969 it disappeared, later coming into the ownership of Keith Barnes in 1986.

Keith spent four years rebuilding the locomotive, providing new nameplates incorporating the MacLeod family crest. He planned for Mac himself to re-name it at the Great Cockcrow Railway, but sadly Alistair passed away the day before the event. Since that time it has been run in Holland, Belgium, Germany and Switzerland and now resides at the Evergreens Miniature Railway in Stickney, Lincolnshire.

Above: Formerly owned by MacLeod, the beautifully restored S160 now operates on the Evergreens Miniature Railway.
(Photo: Keith Barnes)

Right: Close up of the finely detailed MacLeod nameplate. The full name Alistair Balmain MacLeod has been added below the Clan crest.
(Photo: Keith Barnes)

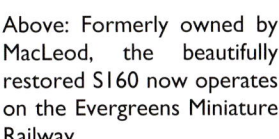

A.B. MACLEOD

Chapter Eleven
Allen and MacLeod

Alistair MacLeod was a popular figure on the lecture circuit and gave profusely illustrated talks to mechanical engineering and enthusiast groups. Some of his lecture notes survive in the Isle of Wight Steam Railway Museum Archive together with an unfinished manuscript for a book entitled *Railways of the Garden Isle*. This appears to have been an ongoing project probably started in the late 1930s, and he was still adding notes in the mid-60s. From the content it is clear that at the time the project was started the only concise work on the Island's railways had been penned by P.C.Allen as *The Railways of the Isle of Wight* in 1928 and, with the rapid changes made to the system by the Southern, this was already out of date at time of publication.

MacLeod first met Peter Allen at Newport in 1930 and their mutual interest was the catalyst for a lifelong friendship. In later years both Allen and MacLeod collaborated on a book *Rails in the Isle of Wight* which was published in 1967. It is now clear that much of Alistair's material and photographs collected for his own book eventually appeared in '*Rails*' and a further publication would have been superfluous at that time. Interestingly, not all of the copy appeared in the final publication; a number of additional appendices on various related subjects were prepared and are now housed in the Isle of Wight Steam Railway's MacLeod archive.

Peter Christopher Allen was born in Ashtead, Surrey, in 1905, and educated at Harrow and Trinity College, Oxford. After graduating in 1928 he joined Brunner Mond, one of four companies which had merged to form Imperial Chemical Industries (ICI) two years earlier, as a research chemist and remained with the Company throughout his career. Appointed a director in 1951 he rose to become Chairman in 1968 following the departure of Richard Beeching. Sir Peter held the Chair until his retirement in 1971 and was knighted for services to his industry in 1967.

PS (2/37)

Southern Railway (London) Lecture and Debating Society

AN
ILLUSTRATED LECTURE

entitled

"THE RAILWAYS OF THE ISLE OF WIGHT"

will be given by

Mr. A. B. MACLEOD,

(Assistant to Loco. Running Superintendent)

at the

Chapter House, St. Thomas' Street,
S.E. 1.

on

Thursday, 4th March, 1937

COMMENCING AT 5.45 p.m.

THE CHAIR WILL BE TAKEN BY

Mr. A. COBB,

(Loco. Running Superintendent)

Visitors will be welcomed. Questions and discussion invited. Membership of the Society is open to all grades of the Company's staff. Visits to places of Transport and General interest are arranged. A Library is available for the use of members.

Heavily involved with the preservation movement, Sir Peter was particularly associated with the National Railway Museum, the Association of Railway Preservation Societies (ARPS) and President of the Transport Trust. Ian Allan wrote in his 1992 book *Driven by Steam*, "*Peter Allen wrote several books for us and inaugurated an annual railway party at his Battle home where he and his wife Consuela entertained every year a wide selection of the cream of railway nuts. It was quite an honour…..I shall remember him best as a genial host each summer in Battle.*"

Left: A page of Mac's original lecture notes.
(A.B.MacLeod collection)

NOTES.

Lecture I.O.W.Railways. Mr.A.B. MacLeod.

1. General.

The peak prewar season was in 1937.   The summer traffic in 1938 and 1939 was affected by the war crises of those years.

2. Wartime Conditions.

(a)   Cessation of summer season traffic 1940 to 1944 inclusive.

(b)   Development of industrial workers traffic from all parts of the Island to Cowes during the same period.

(c)   Development of the Tomato export traffic - upwards of 500 tons annually after the capture of the Channel Islands in 1940.

(d)   Bomb damage at Medina Wharf.

(e)   Closure of the Cement Mills in 1944 and consequent loss of cement and chalk traffic.

3. Post-war conditions.

(a)   The first post war summer service of normal prewar standard introduced on 7th May, 1945, the day of the German surrender.

(b)   Summer Season of 1945 provided record rail traffic within the Island exceeding that of 1937 although intake by boats was about 25% below 1937 level.

4. Engines.

(a)   Stock unchanged since 1939. It is intended to send an E.4 class engine to the Isle of Wight for trial purposes early in 1947.   2510

(b)   Livery.

Wartime livery of unlined black introduced about 1941. Post war livery commenced in the spring of 1945 c.f. photograph No.W.17.

(c)   "Ryde". Mileage on scraping of this engine was 1,556,846. Mileage of old I.W.R. engines at scraping was as follows:-

No. 14.   Shanklin.   1,492,121.
No. 15.   Ventnor.   1,298,310½
No. 16   Wroxall   1,350,674
No. 17   Brading.   1,212,752¼
No. 18   Bonchurch.   1,326,067
            Sandown   1,374,751½

INTRODUCTION

RAILWAYS OF "THE GARDEN ISLE".

The Isle of Wight may be roughly described as being a diamond in shape, about 25 miles long and 14 miles deep.   It is bounded on the N.W.coast by the Solent, on the N.E. coast by Spithead and on the South by the English Channel.

There are two ridges of hills, one running east and west across the centre from Bembridge to the Needles, and one from Shanklin to Chale on the South coast, the highest point being on the top of St Boniface Down, near Ventnor, this is 787 ft. above sea level.

The Isle of Wight has been rightly named "The Garden Isle", with its many marine resorts, each with its own individual climate and natural attractions, its old world villages and the rolling downs offer a great inducement to the tourist of the present day.

It probably appears strange that in an area as small as the Garden Isle, no fewer than six companies have been interested in Railway construction.   It is the intention in this little book to describe briefly these railway interests, including their amalgamation with the Southern Railway Company of England, in 1923.

For the purpose of making the book clear, it has been divided into two parts, the first part being pre-amalgamation and the second after amalgamation up to the present day.

When the Southern Railway under the Grouping Act of 1923 absorbed the railways operating in the Island, there were three distinct Companies who owned their own track, rolling stock and stations.

These were:-

(1)   The Isle of Wight Central Railway which ran from Ryde to Newport, Cowes, Sandown and Ventnor.

(2)   The Isle of Wight Railway, which ran along the East coast from Ryde to Bembridge and Ventnor. Bembridge.

(3)   The Freshwater, Yarmouth and Newport Railway, which ran from Newport to Yarmouth and Freshwater in the West Wight.

The L.B.&.S.C. Railway and the L.& S.W.Railway jointly built a portion of line from Ryde Pier to Ryde,St.Johns Road Station, over which the trains of the Isle of Wight Central and Isle of Wight Railways operated.

These two Companies also jointly worked the steamers between Portsmouth & Southsea and Ryde.   The L.&.S.W.Railway also ran a Steamer from their Pier at Lymington to Yarmouth Pier on the N.W.coast of the Island.

Right: The introduction from MacLeod's draft manuscript for the unpublished *Railways of the Garden Isle*.   (A.B.MacLeod collection)

For some years Alan Blackburn was Chairman of the Isle of Wight Railway Company and the authors asked him his recollections of the Allen – MacLeod involvement in those early days, *"I first met Mac at the Model Railway Club, I had only been a member for a few years but he went back to pre-war years. He was aware of the W.L.S. (Wight Locomotive Society)*, but I don't think he was very impressed. To be honest I think that by this time in his life he was more interested in the GCR than the Island."*

Sir Peter Allen had become involved in the negotiations with Butlins through the ARPS in 1972 when the Isle of Wight Railway Co., along with a number of other preservation groups, had expressed an interest in the acquisition of W11 *Newport*. He was able to secure a long term loan of the engine, in addition providing funding for its cosmetic restoration. Together with MacLeod they supplied drawings for a replica IWCR Wheeler & Hurst chimney and details of livery, both of which were duly applied to W11. As a consequence of these early days Sir Peter became a great friend to the Isle of Wight Steam Railway, a line which he once described as *"his favourite railway."* In later years he negotiated on its behalf for the return of another Terrier locomotive, *Freshwater*, from brewers Whitbread, retrieving the engine from a plinth outside a pub in Hayling Island. Characteristically Uncle Mac was at his side when both locomotives were returned to the Island, together enjoying the various festivities with more than a little touch of nostalgia.

Both MacLeod and Allen were always invited to important functions at the Steam Railway and only ill health precluded attendance on occasions. In consequence of this close association, upon their passing, Mac in 1990 and Sir Peter in 1993, both bequeathed numerous artefacts, photographs and documents to the Steam Railway's Museum. It is from these collections that much of the material in this publication has been sourced.

* *The Wight Locomotive Society was the founding group which purchased locomotive W24 'Calbourne' and six bogie coaches in the Island, later forming The Isle of Wight Railway Co which is the railway operating company trading as Isle of Wight Steam Railway.*

Left: The cover of Peter Allen's 1928 work on the Island Railways.
(Terry Hastings collection)

Welcoming Home W11 *Newport*

ISLE OF WIGHT STEAM RAILWAY

Ryde and Newport Railway

CENTENARY CELEBRATIONS

1875   **1975**

Saturday and Sunday 23/24 August 1975
Havenstreet Station

Souvenir Programme

Mac, along with Peter Allen, was present at a number of significant events in the development of the Isle of Wight Steam Railway. Among these was the arrival of W11 *Newport* back from mainland on 27th January 1973, where it had been in *Butlin's* camp at Pwllheli.

Above Left: W11 arrives back on the Island at Fishbourne to an official welcome. Peter Allen is in the centre, while Mac is centre right in the brown coat. Also present is David Shepherd just behind Mac.

Above Right: Peter Allen on the footplate of W11 at Ryde St Johns Road. The locomotive was delivered here for preliminary restoration work to be carried out and as such was the very last steam engine to enter Ryde Works for attention. Subsequently, *Newport* was transferred to Havenstreet for completion of the task.

Left: A programme signed by Mac, Peter Allen and Lord Montagu of Beaulieu for Centenary Celebrations of the opening of the Ryde and Newport Railway over the August Bank Holiday week-end in 1975. During the Celebration W11 was unveiled cosmetically restored in its IWCR livery.

(Photos: T.Hastings,
Programme: T.Hastings collection)

Left: Through Alistair MacLeod, Peter Allen was able to purchase a selection of Isle of Wight Railway locomotive name and builders plates, photographed at his home shortly after acquisition. On his death, Sir Peter generously bequeathed them to the Isle of Wight Steam Railway's museum.   (Photo: P.C.Allen)

(Above: P.C.Allen collection)

Left: On 22nd January 1976, Lord Mountbatten visited Havenstreet, where he is seen chatting to Sir Peter Allen and Alistair MacLeod, with IWR Company Chairman Alan Blackburn looking on.
          (Photo: P.C.Allen collection)

Chapter Twelve
'My Heart's in the Highlands'

Whilst railways were certainly MacLeod's great love, and particularly those which operated north of the Border, Mac had another passion, again with a Scottish influence. Alistair's son Ewan takes up the story:

"During the 1930s Alistair's father, Dr MacLeod, retired and developed a latent interest in his heritage which percolated down through the family. Alistair and his wife had a postponed honeymoon motoring round the Isle of Skye, the ancient home of the MacLeods, visited Dunvegan Castle and met Dame Flora MacLeod of MacLeod, the chief of the clan. Dr MacLeod co-founded a London Branch of the Clan MacLeod Society in 1937 and became, after WW2, the President. As a consequence Alistair's family were increasingly involved and A.B. acquired a second major life interest, which gave him a great deal of pleasure from this time on.

A multitude of cousins in Scotland and the north of England of whom he had previously only been dimly aware became close and thereafter family visits to Scotland and the activities of the Society became a staple of the annual diary. In due course A.B. succeeded his father as President of the (renamed) Clan MacLeod Society of England, a position he enjoyed for 19 years."

Sadly, after a brief illness, Winifred MacLeod passed away on 27th February 1990, and it was less than six months later, on 3rd August, that Alistair died, quietly at their home in Wimbledon.

The authors felt it was fitting to leave the final words of this book about his father to Ewan MacLeod:

"Both my parents were cremated at Putney Vale Crematorium on Wimbledon Common. Later their caskets were carried by the night sleeper from Euston and were interred in the family Lair in the Western Cemetery, Dundee, where my father's parents and also his grandparents lie. It was drizzling, a damp misty day and a family cousin piped a lament as the caskets were carried by myself and my sister to the lair. The overcast sombre day, very typical of the Isle of Skye, seemed very appropriate for a MacLeod. However, it's a good spot on a sunny day when the view south over the Firth of Tay, taking in the Tay Railway Bridge, is magnificent."

Captured in this photograph of a Clan gathering at the Eccleston Hotel, London, in 1956 are:
(left to right) Alistair MacLeod, Kenneth MacLeod and Dame Flora MacLeod.   (Photo: E.MacLeod collection)

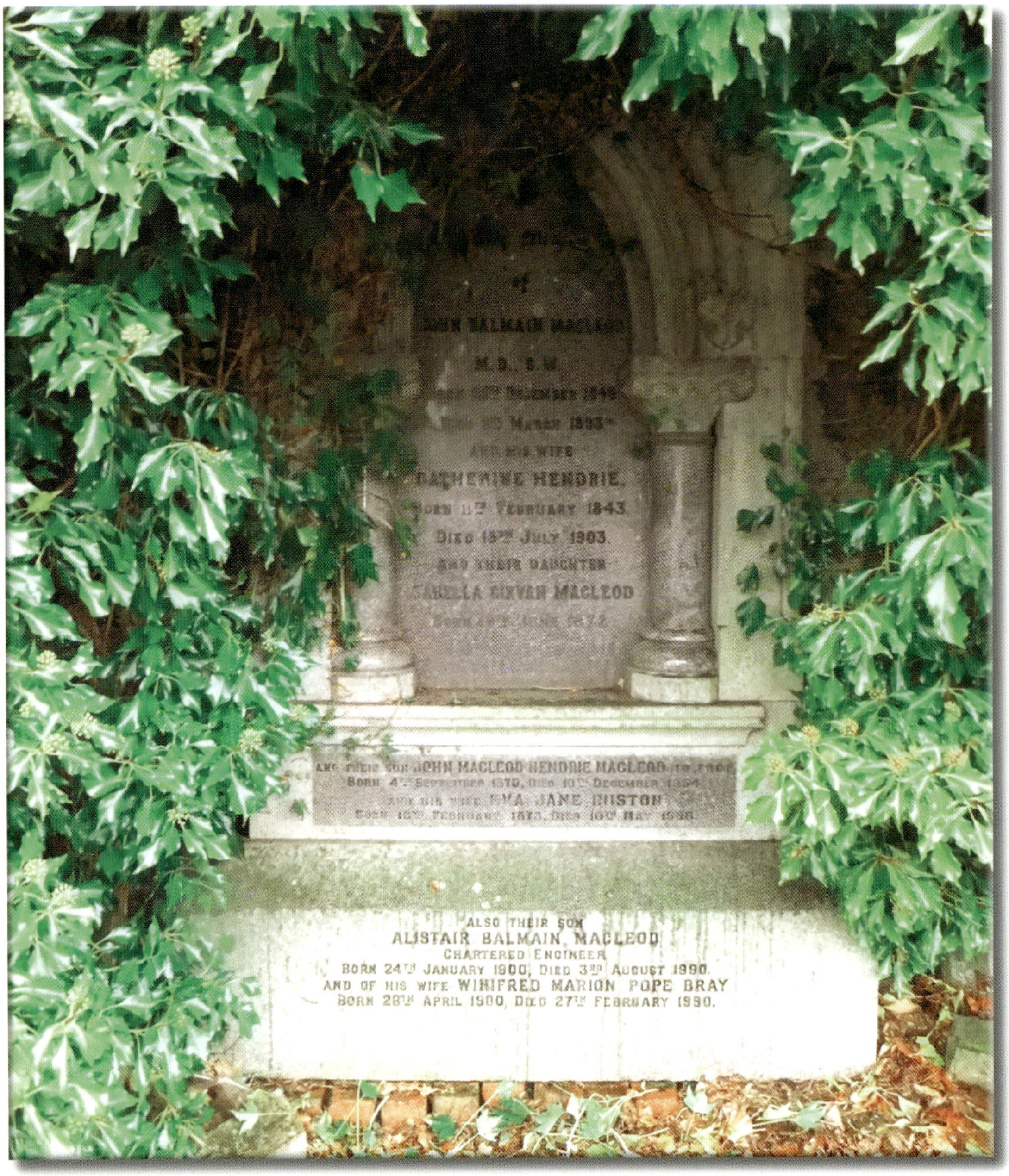
AND HIS WIFE
CATHERINE HENDRIE
AND THEIR DAUGHTER
ALSO THEIR SON
ALISTAIR BALMAIN MACLEOD
CHARTERED ENGINEER
BORN 24TH JANUARY 1900, DIED 3RD AUGUST 1990.
AND OF HIS WIFE WINIFRED MARION POPE BRAY
BORN 28TH APRIL 1900, DIED 27TH FEBRUARY 1990.

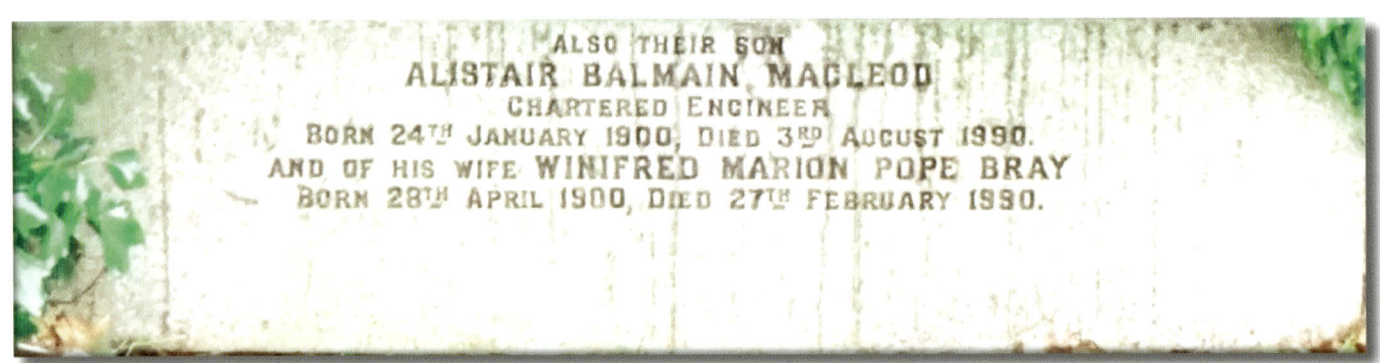

The final resting place of Alistair MacLeod is at the family Lair in the Western Cemetery, Dundee. In an otherwise immaculately maintained cemetery, sadly ivy has encroached from a neighbouring property and been allowed to engulf the MacLeod memorial along with two or three others. March 2011. (Photo: V.B.Orchard)

ALSO THEIR SON
ALISTAIR BALMAIN MACLEOD
CHARTERED ENGINEER
BORN 24TH JANUARY 1900, DIED 3RD AUGUST 1990.
AND OF HIS WIFE WINIFRED MARION POPE BRAY
BORN 28TH APRIL 1900, DIED 27TH FEBRUARY 1990.

Acknowledgements

The authors are particularly indebted to Ewan and Jane MacLeod for their hospitality and allowing access to precious family albums. Ewan has been especially generous with his contributions on personal and family matters.

We are also grateful to Ian and David Allan for permitting access to their photographic library, an interview with David and Ian's suggestion to extract from his autobiography *Driven By Steam*. All extracts reproduced courtesy Ian Allan Publishing.

Richard J.Newman of the Isle of Wight Bus Museum has made available the Minutes of the Southern Railway/ Southern Vectis Standing Joint Committee and also kindly permitted the reproduction of A.B.MacLeod's introduction to Richards book *Southern Vectis - The first 60 Years*.

John Davis and Keith Barnes of the Evergreens Miniature Railway for details of Mac's S160 locomotive.

Dr Alan Doe, for technical assistance and miniature railway information.

Terry Silcock and David Pick of the RCTS for information on the *Ryde* appeal.

Special thanks to Christopher Littledale and his team at the Brighton Toy Museum for access to the MacLeod models, also tolerating our disruption to a busy day.

Alan Blackburn has kindly cast his eye over our efforts and contributed with Mac reminiscences.

The MacLeod Clan Crest and tartan reproduced courtesy of Clan Chief, Hugh MacLeod of MacLeod; also thanks to Mr Sutherland and his staff in Dundee for their assistance with matters tartan.

Thanks to Viv Orchard from co-author Terry Hastings; Viv and his camera came on various expeditions, not least to Dundee when he was forced to travel Standard Class (far below his station) and ended up gardening in cold torrential rain at the Western Cemetery.

Illustrations

The majority of illustrations in this book have come from the collections of Ewan MacLeod, (E.MacLeod collection), and the Isle of Wight Steam Railway Museum's MacLeod Archive, (A.B.MacLeod collection). In all cases where the photographer or supplier of material is known, they too have been acknowledged.

During his time on the Isle of Wight Alistair MacLeod maintained contact with and encouraged eminent railway photographers of the day to visit. MacLeod provided unfettered access to 'his' railway and in exchange was the recipient of numerous examples of their work. Amongst these visitors were O.J.Morris, A.W.Croughton and H.R.Norman, as well as P.C.Allen. Many of their views are in the Museum's MacLeod Archive, much of which was part of his bequest. However, some later appeared as commercial prints from other various sources.

Further Reading

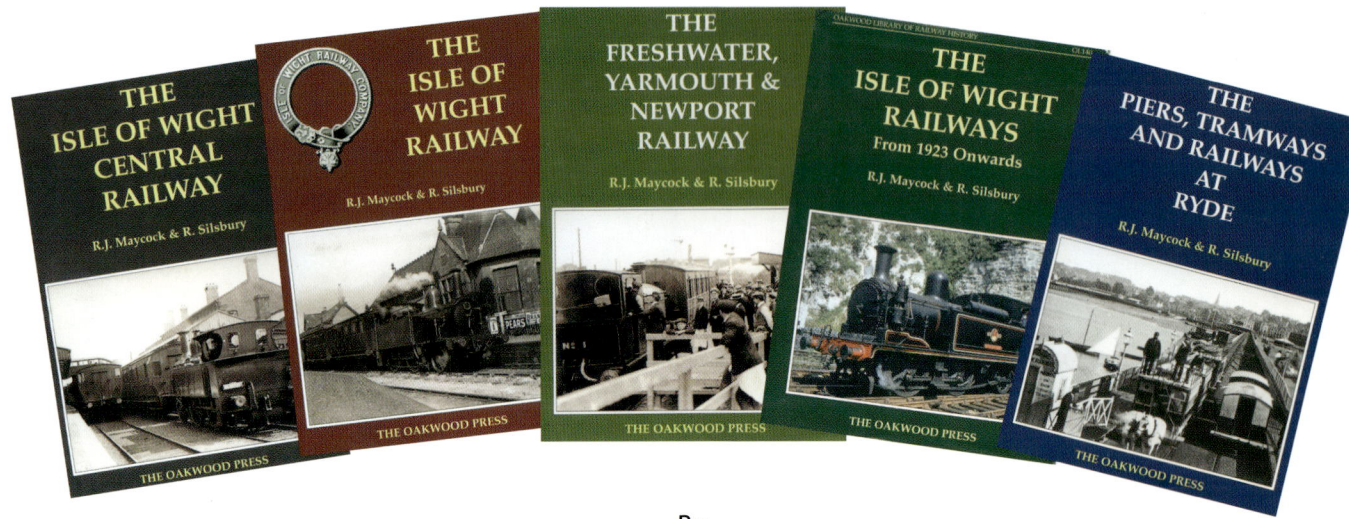

By
Richard Maycock and Roger Silsbury
Published by Oakwood Press

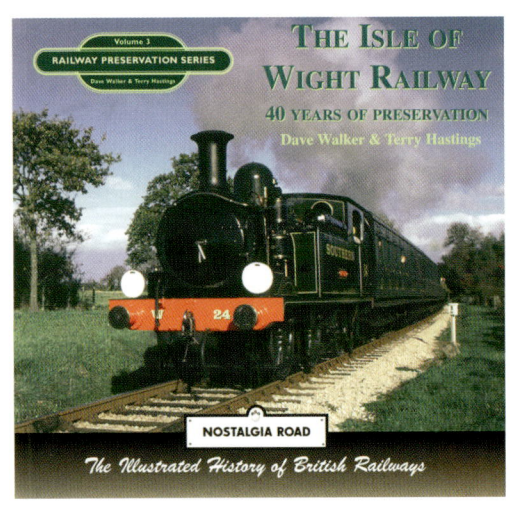

By
Dave Walker and Terry Hastings
Published by
Nostalgia Road Publications

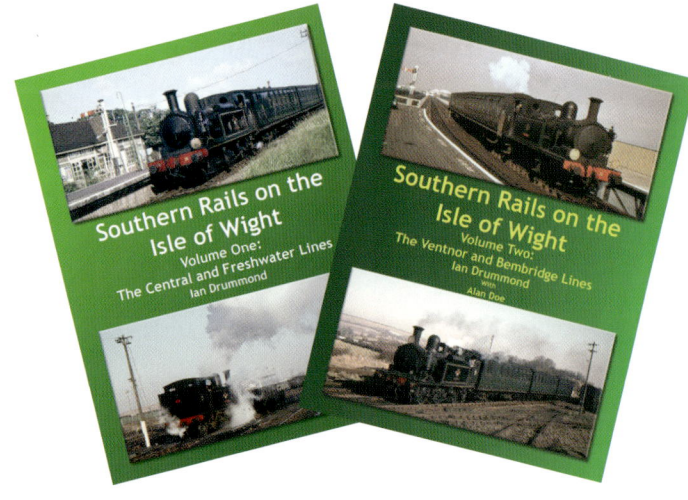

By
Ian Drummond
Published by
Holne Publishing

SOUTHERN RAILW
NUMBERS & CLASSES 'OF ENG

CLASS	TYPE WHEELS	SIZE OF CYL.RS	BOILER PRESSURE	TANK CAPACITY	BRAKE	MAKERS		10	12	4
A'x.	0-6-0 TANK 4'-0"	14" x 20	140 150(4)	500	W.C.	L. B. S. C. R.				
A'x.	0-6-0 TANK 4'-0"	13" x 20"	150	500	W.C.	L. B. S. C. R.	11			
	2-4-0 TANK 3'-6" & 5'-0"	15" x 20"	125	670	W.C.	BEYER PEACOCK & Cº	13			
	2-4-0 TANK 3'-6" & 5'-0"	16" x 20"	125	670	W.C.	BEYER PEACOCK & Cº	16			
02	0-4-4 TANK 4'-10" & 3'-0"	17½" x 24	160	800	W.C.	L. S. W. R.		19 17	20 18	
	0-6-0 TANK 3'-6"	14" x 18	140	600	S.W.	MANNING WARDLE & Cº	1			
A'. Drummond Boiler	0-6-0 TANK 4'-0"	13" x 20"	150	500	W.C.	L. B. S. C. R.	2			
A'x	0-6-0 TANK 4'-0"	12" x 20"	150	500	W.C.	L. B. S. C. R.	3	₩		

1	MEDINA.	13
2	FRESHWATER	
3	CARISBROOKE	
4	BEMBRIDGE.	16
5		17
6		18
5		19
		20
9	FISHBOURNE	2
10	COWES	2
11	NEWPORT	2
12	VENTNOR.	2

W. C. = WESTINGHOUSE BRAKE COMPLETE.

S. W. = STEAM BRAKE & WESTINGHOUSE.